OXFORD

FLASHLIGHT

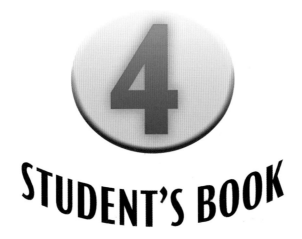

4

STUDENT'S BOOK

Paul A Davies & Tim Falla

FLASHLIGHT CONTENTS

Introduction

WHAT'S IN THIS UNIT?

- Revision: clothes
- Revision: activities
- Personality adjectives
- Present tense contrast
- Revision: past simple affirmative
- Revision: comparative and superlative adjectives
- Revision: *should / shouldn't*
- Talking about arrangements

KELLY'S STORY:

Meet my e-pals!

1 Hi! My name's Jade. I usually wear really casual clothes – jeans with a T-shirt or sweatshirt. I wear a tracksuit when I do sport. (For example, I play basketball after school every Thursday.) But in this photo, I'm wearing more formal clothes – a skirt and a smart top. That's because it's my grandma's birthday and we're all having dinner in an Italian restaurant. The skirt is really old. My mum bought it for me about four years ago. I should get a new one, but I prefer to spend my money on more fashionable clothes when I go shopping! I didn't buy the top, I borrowed it from my sister. She was really angry because I dropped tomato sauce on it. She's so moody!

2 Hello! I'm Chris. At our school, we wear a uniform – dark trousers and a blue sweatshirt. At home, I usually wear a tracksuit and trainers. But in this photo, I'm wearing shorts and a T-shirt. I'm wearing sunglasses too. That's because I'm spending a day at the beach with some friends. We don't go to the beach very often because we don't live near the sea and we're quite lazy! But this was the hottest day of the year, so we took a bus to the coast. We went swimming in the sea and, in the afternoon, we played volleyball on the beach. In the evening, we went to the cinema and saw a great film called "Shy Guy". We didn't get home until midnight. It was a fantastic day.

1 Look at the photos. Describe what the people are wearing.

2 🎧 Read and listen. Where are Jade and Chris in the photos?

3 Answer the questions.

1 What does Jade usually wear?
2 Why is she wearing smart clothes?
3 Why doesn't Jade buy a new skirt?
4 Why did Jade's sister get angry?
5 What does Chris usually wear at home?
6 Why did Chris and his friends go to the beach?
7 What did they do in the afternoon?
8 What did they do in the morning?

4 Bring a photo of yourself into class and talk about it to your partner. Say:

1 what you usually wear
2 what you're wearing in the photo
3 where you are / what you're doing in the photo
4 anything else you remember about that day

> I usually wear ... but in this photo I'm wearing ... because ...

> It was a (great / fantastic / terrible / embarrassing) day. We ...

VOCABULARY

Revision: clothes

1 Which of these items of clothing can you find (a) in the photos on page 4 and (b) in the texts?

cap dress jacket jeans shorts skirt
socks sweatshirt top T-shirt
tracksuit trainers trousers

2 Work in pairs. Ask and answer about people in your class.

1 What are you wearing?
2 What's the teacher wearing?
3 What is … wearing?

Revision: activities

3 Match the words with the pictures.

listen to music play volleyball
go to the cinema play computer games
read magazines surf the Internet
meet friends go shopping

4 Write sentences with *often*, *sometimes*, *hardly ever* or *never* and the activities in exercise 3.

I hardly ever play computer games.
I often play volleyball.

Adjectives to describe personality

5 🎧 Listen and repeat the adjectives in the boxes.

A cheerful generous hard-working
loud nice serious shy

B confident funny lazy mean
moody nasty quiet

6 Match adjectives in A with adjectives in B to make six more pairs of opposites.

cheerful – moody

7 Write four sentences describing yourself, your friends and members of your family. Use three adjectives in each sentence.

I think I'm ……, …… and …….
My brother is …….

8 Look at the pictures. Describe the people. Use adjectives from exercise 5.

1 I think he's …

More practice?   Workbook page 72

GRAMMAR 1

Present tense contrast

Watch out!

We use the present continuous for actions that are happening now.

Look! It's raining.

We use the present simple for actions that happen regularly or always.

It often rains in February.

1 Complete the sentences. Use the present simple or present continuous.

1 a) Be quiet! I ...... to the radio. (listen)
   b) I always ...... to the radio in bed. (listen)
2 a) He ...... school uniform today. (not wear)
   b) He ...... trainers during the week. (not wear)
3 a) Look! It .... (snow)
   b) It never ...... in Egypt. (snow)
4 a) We ...... a computer at home. (not use)
   b) We ...... our car at the moment. (not use)

2 🎧 Complete the phone conversation between Rob and Chris. Use the present simple or present continuous. Then listen and check.

Rob Hi, Chris. Where are you?

Chris I'm in a music shop. I (**1** look) for a birthday present for Mum. (**2** you / play) football?

Rob No, I'm not. I (**3** not play) football on Saturdays. It's basketball today!

Chris Oh right. (**4** you / win)?

Rob Yes, we are.

Chris Good! Look, I've got a question. (**5** Mum / like) Shakira?

Rob Yes, she does. She's got all her CDs.

Chris OK. Thanks!

Revision: past simple affirmative (regular verbs)

3 Study the table and answer the questions.

Affirmative (regular)
I **listened** to the radio last night. We **lived** in London from 2002 to 2005. My sister **studied** French at school. I **chatted** to my friends for hours.

Affirmative (irregular)
I **went** to the cinema last night. Chelsea **won** the match.
We use the past simple to talk about completed actions in the past.

1 What does the past simple affirmative of regular verbs end in?
2 Is the past simple form the same for every person?

Watch out

There aren't any spelling rules for irregular verbs. You have to learn them.

4 Complete the text with the past simple affirmative. Which verbs are irregular?

I **had** (have) a good day yesterday. I (**1** arrive) at school on time. I (**2** get) good marks in science. My friend in Australia (**3** phone) me at lunchtime. I (**4** play) football after school and we (**5** win). In the evening, my sister (**6** tidy) her bedroom and (**7** find) my trainers in there! My mum (**8** cook) dinner for me. After dinner, I (**9** listen) to music with the girl next door, and we (**10** chat) about our favourite bands.

More practice? **Workbook pages 73–74**

Dialogue

1 🎧 **Read and listen. What is the arrangement?**

a) They're going to the cinema at seven o'clock this evening.

b) They're meeting some friends in a café.

c) They're seeing a film on Saturday evening.

Talking about arrangements

Harry	Hi, Sarah. This is Harry. How are you?
Sarah	I'm well, thanks. And you?
Harry	I'm fine. Listen, are you doing anything on Saturday evening?
Sarah	I don't think so. Why?
Harry	I'm going to the cinema with some friends. They're showing the new Will Smith film. Do you want to come?
Sarah	Yes, please. I'd love to. Thanks!
Harry	Why don't we ask Kelly, too?
Sarah	Oh, OK. I'm seeing her tomorrow at school. I can ask her then.
Harry	Great! We're meeting outside the cinema at seven o'clock.
Sarah	OK. See you there!

Take note!

We can use the present continuous to talk about future arrangements.

Are you **doing** anything next weekend?

I'**m seeing** my grandparents on Sunday.

2 **REAL ENGLISH** 🎧 **Listen and repeat these expressions from the dialogue.**

1 This is Harry.
2 I'm well, thanks.
3 I don't think so.
4 I'd love to.

3 **Practise reading the dialogue.**

4 **Write your own dialogue. Choose one of these arrangements.**

> going bowling   playing football in the park
> having a barbecue on the beach
> watching a DVD

> A: Hi, ... This is .... How are you?
> B: I'm well, thanks. And you?

5 **Act out your dialogue.**

Listening

6 🎧 **Listen to Sarah and Kelly. Why can't Sarah go to the cinema?**

7 🎧 **Listen again. Choose a or b.**

1 Kelly is …
   a) on the bus.
   b) at the bus stop.
2 The time is …
   a) ten to seven.
   b) ten past seven.
3 Sarah's mum is …
   a) working.
   b) looking after Luke.
4 Sarah's grandma is …
   a) working.
   b) visiting a friend.
5 Sarah can't call Harry because …
   a) she hasn't got his mobile phone number.
   b) she hasn't got a mobile phone.

More practice?	Workbook page 75

GRAMMAR 2

Revision: comparative and superlative adjectives

1 Complete the table.

Adjective	Comparative	Superlative
quiet	quieter (than)	the quietest
nice	(1) ...... (than)	the nicest
big	bigger (than)	(2) ......
funny	(3) ...... (than)	the funniest
serious	(4) ...... (than)	the most serious
cheerful	more cheerful (than)	(5) ......
good	(6) ......(than)	the best
bad	worse (than)	(7) ......

2 Compare the characters from the story. Write four sentences with comparative adjectives and four with superlatives. Choose from the adjectives in the box.

> beautiful cheerful competitive confident
> funny hard-working intelligent quiet shy

I think Kelly is more
...... than ....
I think Sarah is
the most ....

Revision: *should / shouldn't*

3 Complete the chart. Is the third person (he/she/it) form different?

Affirmative: *should*
I should go now.
She should go now.
We (2) ...... go now.

Negative: *shouldn't*
You shouldn't go now.
He (2) ...... go now.
They shouldn't go now.

Interrogative: *should ...?*
(3) ...... I go now?
Yes, you should. / No, you shouldn't.
Should she go now?
Yes, she should. / No, she (4) ....

4 Look at the pictures. Write questions and answers with *should*.

wear a coat?
Should he wear a coat? Yes, he should.

1 buy some new shoes?

2 play in the street?

3 take an umbrella with him?

4 go to the doctor's?

5 copy her friend's homework

More practice?   Workbook pages 73–74

1 Incredible journeys

VOCABULARY

Transport

1 🎧 Match the words with the pictures. Then listen and repeat.

bike   bus   car   underground   plane   helicopter   boat   motorbike   moped   train   ship

> **Take note!**
>
> go by bus, by car, by train, etc.
> I go to school **by** bus.

2 🎧 Listen. How do these teenagers get to school? Complete *A Transport*.

	A Transport	B Time
1 Beth	walks	5 minutes
2 David		
3 Robert		
4 Linda		
5 Christina		

3 🎧 Listen again. How long does it take? Complete *B Time*.

4 In pairs, ask and answer.

> How do you get to school?

> I go to school by ... / I walk to school.

> How long does it take?

> Ten minutes.

| More practice? | Workbook page 76 |

SARAH'S STORY

Harry isn't a thief!

1 When I go into town, I usually cycle. It's slower than the bus, but it's cheaper – and anyway, there isn't a bus stop near my house. When I was in town last Saturday, I stopped outside a music shop to look at a poster in the window. Then I saw Harry inside. He had headphones on and a CD in his hand. He didn't notice me at first, so I shouted …

Harry! Harry! Over here!

Harry

I wanna heal, I wanna feel what I thought was never real!

2 At last, Harry noticed me. He didn't take off the headphones or put down the CD. He just ran out of the shop. A really loud alarm started ringing. Then a security guard appeared. Harry didn't know why – but I guessed …

What a terrible noise!

Hey you!

It started when you left the shop. Did you pay for that CD?

3 Harry tried to explain, but the security guard didn't believe him. Poor Harry – he was really embarrassed!

I didn't steal it! I saw my friend outside and…

This way, please.

4 It was OK in the end. I went into the shop and explained. Harry paid for the CD and we left. Harry didn't catch the bus home or underground. We walked together. He was still really embarrassed, but I couldn't stop laughing!

1 🎧 Read and listen. Which three forms of transport does Sarah mention?

2 Put the events in the correct order.

    a Harry ran out of the shop.
    b Harry and Sarah walked home.
    c Sarah saw Harry.
    d A security guard appeared.
    e An alarm started ringing.
    g Harry paid for the CD.

3 **REAL ENGLISH** Who says these expressions? What do they mean?

    1 Over here!   2 Hey you!

    3 Poor Harry.   4 This way, please.

Teen focus

Vandalism
Read what Harry says about vandalism. Is there much vandalism where you live?

There isn't much vandalism in our town. Sometimes people spray graffiti on walls, and last year some boys smashed a shop window, but the police caught them.

Word check Travel words

4 Complete the story with the travel words in the box.

> arrived bus stop caught left stop
> tickets

Last week Sarah, Kelly and Harry went to a music festival. They (**1**) ...... home early in the morning. They went to the train station and bought their (**2**) .... They (**3**) ...... the train at 10.13, but it didn't (**4**) ...... at Bampton. They walked to a (**5**) ...... and waited for a bus. They (**6**) ...... at the music festival at three o'clock.

More practice?	Workbook page 76

Study skills

Learning irregular verb forms

5 Complete the past simple of these irregular verbs. Use the list on page 103. Can you see any patterns?

base form	past simple
bring	brought
think	_____
teach	_____
catch	_____
sit	sat
swim	_____
sing	_____
drink	_____

6 Using the list, find one more verb that follows a similar pattern to each of these verbs:

> know tell break lend

GRAMMAR 1

Past simple negative and interrogative

1 Study the table.

Negative
I **didn't watch** TV last night.
He **didn't see** a film.

Interrogative
Did she **watch** TV last night?
Did you **see** a film?

Short answers
Yes, she **did**. / No, she **didn't**.
Yes, I **did**. / No, I **didn't**.

Full forms
didn't = did not
We use the past simple to talk about completed actions in the past.

2 Complete the rules. Use *did* and *didn't*.

1 We form the negative of all verbs with ......
+ base form.
2 We form the interrogative of all verbs with
...... + subject + base form.

3 Complete the sentences. Use the past simple negative.

Columbus didn't want (not want) to go to America in 1492, he wanted to go to China.
1 The explorer Marco Polo ...... (not visit) Australia, he visited China.
2 In 1961, the Russian astronaut Yuri Gagarin went into space, but he ...... (not go) to the moon.
3 The explorer Hernán Cortés ...... (not come) from Portugal, he came from Spain.
4 The explorer James Cook ...... (not discover) Australia in 1770, but he explored it.
5 The Titanic ...... (not arrive) in the USA in 1912 because it sank in the Atlantic Ocean.

More practice?   Workbook pages 77–78

4 Complete the text about the explorer Shackleton. Use the past simple negative.

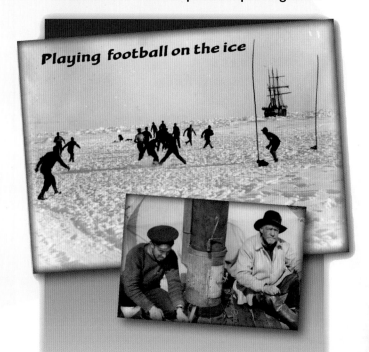

Playing football on the ice

In 1915, Shackleton started an incredible journey – to cross Antarctica. Shackleton and 27 men travelled south in a ship called *Endurance*, but they (**1**) ...... (not get) to Antarctica because the sea was full of ice. They (**2**) ...... (not move) for 11 months! Then *Endurance* sank, but the men (**3**) ...... (not die) because they reached a small island called Elephant Island. They (**4**) ...... (not have) much food, so they ate penguins. They (**5**) ...... (not see) any ships, so Shackleton and five men left the island in a small boat. It was a very dangerous journey, but the boat (**6**) ...... (not sink). They travelled 1,280 kilometres before they found help.

5 Put the words in the correct order to make questions about Shackleton's journey. Then write answers.

he / in 1915? / Did / start / his journey
Did he start his journey in 1915?
Yes, he did.
1 get / they / Antarctic? / Did / to / the
2 sink? / *Endurance* / Did
3 a lot of / have / food? / they / Did
4 penguins? / Did / eat / they
5 leave / Did / Elephant Island? / Shackleton
6 help? / Shackleton / Did / find

Dialogue

1 🎧 Read and listen. Are the sentences true or false?

1 Joe wants to go to London.
2 He's coming back.
3 The ticket is £5.
4 The train leaves from platform 4.

AT THE TRAIN STATION

Joe	Can I have a ticket to Bolton, please?
Clerk	Single or return?
Joe	Return.
Clerk	That's £15, please.
Joe	Which platform is it?
Clerk	Number four. The next train is at ten past eleven.
Joe	Thanks.
Clerk	You're welcome.

2 🎧 Listen and repeat the phrases from the dialogue.

1 Single or return?
2 Which platform is it?
3 You're welcome.

3 Practise reading the dialogue.

4 Write your own dialogue. Use places on the map on page 66 to help you.

A: Can I have … ?
B: Single … ?
A: …
B: That's …
A: Which … ?
B: Number … The next …
A: Thanks.
B: You're …

5 In pairs, act out your dialogue.

Can I have … ?

Single … ?

More practice? ▸ Workbook page 79

Listening

6 🎧 Listen to the three conversations (1–3). Complete the chart with the places in the box.

Luton   London   Liverpool

	Place
1	
2	
3	

7 🎧 Listen again. Copy and complete the chart.

Conversation	1	2	3
Single or return?	*single*		
Price of ticket			
Platform number			
Time of departure			

8 **MAPS** Find Bolton, Luton, London and Liverpool on the map on page 66.

Past simple revision

1 Complete the conversation. Use the past simple affirmative, negative and interrogative.

Anna	Where **did** you **go** (go) on holiday?
Harry	We (**1**) ...... (go) to Egypt.
Anna	Really? (**2**) ...... you ...... (enjoy) it?
Harry	Yes, we had a great time.
Anna	Who (**3**) ...... you ...... (go) with?
Harry	My mum and dad. My little brother (**4**) ...... (not go). He stayed with my grandparents.
Anna	(**5**) ...... you ...... (see) the Pyramids?
Harry	Yes, we did. And we took a boat trip on the Nile.
Anna	(**6**) ...... you ...... (take) any photos?
Harry	No, I didn't. I (**7**) ...... (not have) my camera. But I bought this for you – it's a model of a pyramid!

Communicate!

Write and ask your partner three questions about last weekend.

What did you do on ... ?

Where ... ?

Pronunciation The sounds /b/ and /v/

2 🎧 Listen. Pay attention to the sounds.

/b/	bus	baby	boat
/v/	video	visit	very

3 🎧 Listen and repeat the sentence. Can you say it three times in ten seconds?

Bill's brother Vince visited Barbados by boat.

Prepositions of movement

4 Look at the pictures and the prepositions.

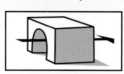
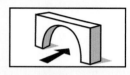

1 through   2 under

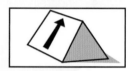

3 across   4 up

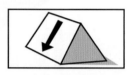

5 over   6 down

5 Complete the sentences. Use the prepositions of movement in exercise 4.

1 He climbed ...... the mountain.

2 He walked ...... a bridge.

3 He climbed ...... a wall.

4 He walked ...... a tunnel.

5 He went ...... the mountain.

6 He skied ...... the ice.

More practice?	Workbook pages 77–78

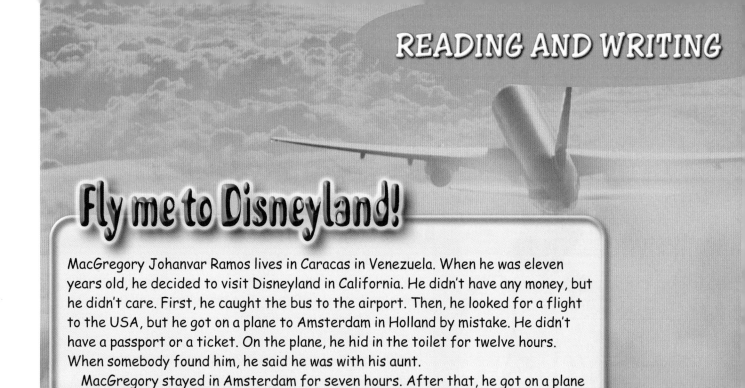

Fly me to Disneyland!

MacGregory Johanvar Ramos lives in Caracas in Venezuela. When he was eleven years old, he decided to visit Disneyland in California. He didn't have any money, but he didn't care. First, he caught the bus to the airport. Then, he looked for a flight to the USA, but he got on a plane to Amsterdam in Holland by mistake. He didn't have a passport or a ticket. On the plane, he hid in the toilet for twelve hours. When somebody found him, he said he was with his aunt.

MacGregory stayed in Amsterdam for seven hours. After that, he got on a plane to Budapest in Hungary. Again, nobody checked his ticket! When he arrived in Budapest, the police arrested him and put him in a hotel. Finally, they sent him back to Caracas. Why did he do it? Nobody knows, but it was probably for fun!

Reading

1 🎧 Read the text. Answer the questions.

1 Where did he decide to visit?
2 How did he get to the airport?
3 Did he get on a plane to the USA?
4 Where did he hide on the plane?
5 How long did he stay in Amsterdam?
6 What happened when he arrived in Budapest?

2 MAPS Find or mark the cities that MacGregory visited on the map on pages 68–9.

Writing Ordering events

> **Take note!**
>
> We use these words to order events.
> first   then   after that   finally

3 Rewrite the paragraph. Use the words from the *Take note!* box.

> Last winter I went to Britain with my family. We visited London. We took the train to Oxford and visited the university. We took a plane to Scotland. We spent a few days in Wales.

4 Imagine that you went on an incredible journey. Choose three places and mark them on the map on pages 68–9. Then complete the chart below with the cities and forms of transport.

	To (city)	**By** (transport)
First		
Then		
After that		
Finally	(your home)	

5 Write about your journey. Use the chart and writing plan to help you.

> Last summer I went on an incredible journey.
> First, I went to ... by ...
> When I arrived, I ... (What did you do?)
> Then I went to ... by ...
> The journey took ... (How long?)
> After that, I went to ... by ...
> I stayed there for ... (How long?)
> I saw ... (What did you see?)
> Finally, I caught the ... back to ...

More practice?   **Workbook pages 79–80**

FOCUS ON THE WORLD

1 🎧 Read the texts and match them to the maps.

Explorers

FERNAND MAGELLAN.

1

In 1519, Ferdinand Magellan, a Portuguese explorer, wanted to travel around the world. He left Spain with five ships and about 260 men. But Magellan didn't finish the journey. He died in April 1521. Only one ship came back to Spain. The eighteen men on that ship were the first people to travel around the world.

2

Robert Scott, an English explorer, wanted to be the first person to get to the South Pole. In 1910, Scott and his men started their journey from New Zealand. They arrived at the South Pole in January 1912. But they weren't the first at the Pole. Amundsen, a Norwegian explorer, arrived there in December 1911. The weather became very bad and Scott and his men couldn't get home. They died in Antarctica in March 1912.

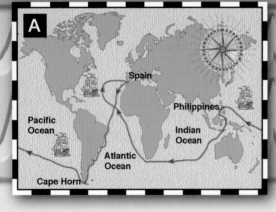

A

Spain
Philippines
Pacific Ocean
Indian Ocean
Atlantic Ocean
Cape Horn

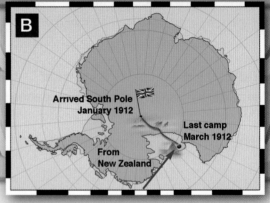

B

Arrived South Pole January 1912
Last camp March 1912
From New Zealand

2 Read the questions. Write answers for Magellan and Scott.

What nationality was he?
Magellan was Portuguese. Scott was English.

1 When did he start his journey?
2 Where did he start his journey from?
3 What did he want to do?
4 Did he return home?
5 When did he die?

Song and Reading File page 57.

2 Mystery

WHAT'S IN THIS UNIT?

- In the home
- Parts of a house
- Past continuous
- Asking for and giving permission
- *so*

VOCABULARY

In the home

1 🎧 Listen and repeat.

2 Where are these things in the picture? Write sentences with *in*, *on*, *under* or *next to*.

Where's the notebook?
It's under the sofa.

1 letter   4 photo
2 pen   5 key
3 coin

3 In pairs, ask and answer about your classroom. Use the words from exercise 1.

Is there a sofa in the classroom?

No, there isn't.

More practice?   Workbook page 81

1 Last week Harry invited me to go to a party. I was really excited about it. But then, on the day of the party, my mum was feeling ill. She works at Freddy's Diner in town, but she couldn't go, so I worked for her. It's a nice café, and Freddy is a good boss – but I hate going down to the basement. There are lights and mirrors in the café, but the basement is really cold and dark. It's spooky!

> Sarah, can you put these chips in the freezer in the basement? Be careful – it's dark down there.

Harry

2 I put the chips in the freezer. While I was going up the stairs, I'm sure I heard a voice. It was saying my name. Or was I imagining it? I felt scared and ran back to the kitchen. I started cooking some chips, but I wasn't concentrating on my work - I was thinking about the voice in the basement!

3 When I turned round, Harry was coming out of the bathroom. Freddy was looking at us and he was smiling.

> It's quiet tonight Sarah. Why don't you leave with your friend?

> Let's go to the party!

> Better late than never!

1 🎧 Read and listen. Does Sarah work all evening?

2 Correct the sentences.

1 **Kelly** invited Sarah to go to a party.
2 Sarah couldn't go to the party because her **brother** was ill.
3 Sarah worked for her mum in a **shop**.
4 It was **light and warm** downstairs by the freezer.
5 Sarah was thinking about **her work**.
6 Freddy let Sarah and Harry go to the **cinema**.

3 REAL ENGLISH Who says these expressions? What do they mean?

1 It's spooky.

2 Be careful.

3 Let's go to the party!

4 Better late than never!

Teen focus

Eating out
Read what Sarah says about eating out. How often do you eat out?

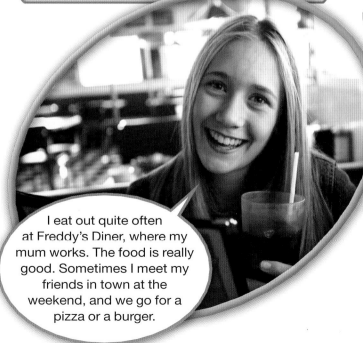

I eat out quite often at Freddy's Diner, where my mum works. The food is really good. Sometimes I meet my friends in town at the weekend, and we go for a pizza or a burger.

Word check Parts of a house

4 Match the words in the box with six of the pictures. Find three other missing parts of the house in the story.

garden   bedroom   living room   hall
dining room   toilet

 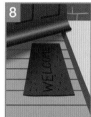 

| More practice? | Workbook page 81 |

Study skills

Using pictures

5 Some vocabulary sets are easier to learn if you draw and label a picture. Which of these sets are suitable, in your opinion?

days of the week   objects in a classroom
parts of the body   clothes
adjectives to describe personality

6 Choose one of the sets from Exercise 5. Draw and label a picture.

GRAMMAR 1

Past continuous

1 Study the table. What are the full forms of the past continuous negative?

Affirmative	Negative
I was laughing	I wasn't laughing
you were laughing	you weren't laughing
he was laughing	he wasn't laughing
she was laughing	she wasn't laughing
it was laughing	it wasn't laughing
we were laughing	we weren't laughing
you were laughing	you weren't laughing
they were laughing	they weren't laughing

We use the past continuous for actions that were in progress at a specific moment in the past.

2 Write sentences. Use the past continuous affirmative.

She / watch / TV / at nine o'clock last night
She was watching TV at nine o'clock last night.

1 We / have / dinner / at seven o'clock last night
2 I / sit / in the living room/ at midnight
3 You / do / your homework / at five o'clock on Sunday
4 My sister / chat / to her friend / at eleven o'clock last night
5 You / study / at nine o'clock yesterday
6 They / shop / at ten o'clock this morning

3 Complete the sentences. Use the past continuous negative.

1 We …… (not do) our homework at four o'clock.
2 It was a hot afternoon, so she …… (not run).
3 You …… (not listen) to the teacher!
4 They …… (not play) football at six o'clock.
5 The music was terrible, so we …… (not dance).
6 My sister …… (not watch) TV at eight o'clock.

| **More practice?** | **Workbook pages 82–83** |

4 Look at the photo and write sentences. Use the past continuous affirmative and negative.

Scully / not wear / a T-shirt, she / wear / a white jacket
Scully wasn't wearing a T-shirt, she was wearing a white jacket.

1 Mulder / not wear / a T-shirt. He / wear / a shirt
2 Mulder / not look at / Scully, he / look at / the alien
3 Scully and Mulder / not sit / they / stand
4 The alien / not look at / Scully / he / sleep

5 Complete the text with the verbs in the box. Use the past continuous affirmative and negative.

| not rain   sit   swim   walk   not watch |
| ~~stay~~   write |

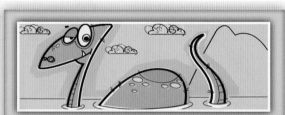

Last month, I went to Scotland with my mum and dad. We were staying in a hotel near Loch Ness. One day, I (**1**) …… along the road next to the loch. It was cold and cloudy, but it (**2**) …… .

Suddenly, I saw a strange animal in the water. It (**3**) …… very fast. I ran to the hotel. My mum and dad (**4**) …… in the living room. The TV was on, but they (**5**) …… it. They (**6**) …… postcards. I told them about the strange animal. We all went to the loch, but the animal wasn't there.

Dialogue

1 🎧 Read and listen. Complete the dialogue with the words in the box.

> idea   cinema   OK   not

ASKING FOR AND
GIVING PERMISSION

Alex Can I go to the (**1**) ...... with Joe this evening?

Dad Yes, sure. That's a nice (**2**) ....

Alex Great! Can we go to the Internet café after the film?

Dad No, you can't. Sorry.

Alex Why (**3**) ...... ?

Dad Because it's Monday evening. You've got school tomorrow.

Alex Oh, (**4**) ....

2 🎧 Listen and repeat the phrases from the dialogue.

1 Can I go to the cinema?
2 Can we go to the Internet café?
3 Why not?

3 Practise reading the dialogue.

4 Write your own dialogue. Use the ideas in the box to help you or use your own ideas.

Ideas for A	Ideas for B
invite my friend to my house?	Yes
play football in the garden?	No (it's raining)
phone my friend in England?	Yes
go to London this afternoon?	No (you've got a lot of homework)

A: Can I ... ?
B: Yes ... That's ...
A: Great! Can we ... ?
B: No ...
A: Why ...?
B: Because ...
A: Oh, ...

5 Act out your dialogue.

> Can I ... ?

> Yes ... That's ...

> **More practice?**   **Workbook page 84**

Listening

6 🎧 Listen. Who is Alex talking to?

Conversation 1: He's talking to his ...
Conversation 2: He's talking to his ...
Conversation 3: He's talking to his ...

7 🎧 Listen again. Choose the correct answers.

1 Alex's sister is watching:
   a) a soap opera b) a chat show
2 Alex can watch a DVD in the:
   a) bedroom b) dining room
3 Alex 's grandad was born in:
   a) 1942 b) 1952
4 Alex wants to take the photos to:
   a) his friend's house b) his school
5 Alex wants to wear a hat and jacket because:
   a) he likes the colour b) it's very cold

GRAMMAR 2

Past continuous interrogative

1 Study the table.

Affirmative	Interrogative
I was laughing	Was I laughing …?
you were laughing	Were you laughing …?
he was laughing	Was he laughing …?
she was laughing	Was she laughing …?
it was laughing	Was it laughing …?
we were laughing	Were we laughing …?
you were laughing	Were you laughing …?
they were laughing	Were they laughing …?

Short answers
Yes, I was. / No, I wasn't.
Yes, we were. / No, we weren't.

2 Look at the picture. Write questions and short answers.

At eight o'clock last night …

Megan / watch / TV
Was Megan watching TV?
No, she wasn't.

1 Sophie and Charlie / watch / TV
2 Tom and Charlie / sit / on the floor
3 Charlie / eat / crisps
4 Megan / read / a magazine
5 Sophie / eat / crisps
6 Tom / read a book

3 Write questions about these times.

you / five o'clock yesterday morning?
What were you doing at five o'clock yesterday morning?

1 you / at eleven o'clock yesterday morning?
2 you / at two o'clock yesterday afternoon?
3 your best friend / at four o'clock yesterday afternoon?
4 your cousin / at six o'clock yesterday?
5 your parents / nine o'clock last night?
6 your class / half past nine yesterday morning?

4 In pairs, ask and answer the questions in exercise 3.

> What were you doing at five o'clock yesterday morning?

Communicate!

Ask a partner what they were doing at these times yesterday?
8 am 1 pm 5 pm 8 pm 11.30 pm
At 8 am I was going to school.
At 1 pm I …

More practice?	Workbook pages 82–83

Pronunciation Weak forms /wəz/, /wə(r)/

5 🎧 Listen and repeat. Pay attention to the weak forms of *was* and *were*.

1 It *was* raining this morning.
2 My brother *was* dancing with his friend.
3 You *were* running.
4 I *was* walking along the road.
5 We *were* staying in a hotel.
6 We *were* sitting on the sofa.

A Strange Experience

Last month, I was on holiday in Ireland with my mum and dad. One day, we were driving through a small village. It was time for lunch, so we stopped at a restaurant.

It was a large, old building. We looked through the window. There were lots of people in the restaurant. They were eating, drinking and chatting. A musician was playing the violin. But there was something strange about the people. They weren't wearing normal, modern clothes. They were wearing hats, jackets and dresses from another century. We couldn't understand it. But we were hungry, so we opened the door.

When we went into the restaurant, everything was different. The people were wearing normal clothes. The musician wasn't there – the music was on CD. It was a very strange experience!

Daniel

Reading

1 🎧 Read Daniel's story. Answer the questions.

1 Who was Daniel on holiday with?
2 Why did they stop at a restaurant?
3 What were the people in the restaurant doing?
4 What instrument was the musician playing?
5 What was strange about their clothes?
6 When they went into the restaurant, did they see the musician?

Writing *so*

Take note!

We use *so* to join ideas together and explain a consequence.

It was cold. I closed the window.
It was cold, **so** I closed the window.

2 Match sentences (1–5) with sentences (a–e). Write the sentences and join them together with *so*.

1 – c It was late, so we went home.

1	It was late.	a)	I went to bed.
2	She was hungry.	b)	He caught a bus.
3	He couldn't drive.	c)	We went home.
4	I was tired.	d)	I went swimming.
5	It was hot.	e)	She bought a pizza.

3 Write a story. Use the picture and the writing plan to help you.

Last year, I was on holiday in ... with ...
We were driving through ...
It was late, so we stopped at a hotel.
We looked through the window.
There were ...
We opened the door and ...
Everything was ... The people ...
It was a ... experience.

More practice?   Workbook pages 84–85

1 🎧 Read the text.

2 **MAPS** Look at the map of the Bermuda Triangle. Which continent is it near?

The Bermuda Triangle

It was a sunny afternoon in 1945. Five American planes were flying over the sea near Florida. Everything was fine. Suddenly, the pilots sent a strange message to their controllers: 'This is an emergency. We're lost.'

'Fly west,' the controllers said. The pilots sent this answer:

'Everything is wrong – strange. We aren't sure of any direction. The sea looks different.'

Then the five planes disappeared. The pilots' last words were: 'We are completely lost.' The controllers sent another plane to look for the pilots. That plane disappeared too.

Soon, people were talking about the 'Bermuda Triangle'. Strange things happen in this part of the ocean. For example, an American ship called the USS Cyclops disappeared. There were 300 men on the ship. The weather was sunny. The ship did not send any messages. Where did it go? Nobody knows. The Bermuda Triangle is a mystery.

3 Answer the questions.

1 When did five American planes disappear?
2 Was it raining when they disappeared?
3 Why did the controllers send another plane?
4 What happened to the other plane?
5 What was the USS Cyclops?
6 Did the USS Cyclops send any messages?

Song and Reading File page 57.

VOCABULARY

Clothes and personality adjectives

1 Put the words in the correct groups.

> cap cheerful confident dress funny
> generous hard-working jacket jeans
> lazy loud mean moody nasty nice
> quiet serious shorts shy skirt socks
> sweatshirt top T-shirt tracksuit
> trainers trousers

Clothes	Personality adjectives
cap	cheerful

Activities

2 Complete the activities. Use the words in the box.

> the cinema computer games friends
> the Internet magazines music
> shopping volleyball

1 play …   4 go to …   7 meet …
2 listen to … 5 read …   8 go …
3 play …   6 surf …

Transport

3 Label the pictures. Use the words in the box.

> underground plane helicopter boat
> motorbike moped train ship

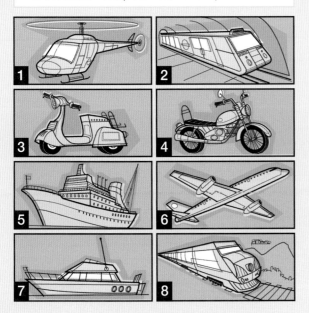

Travel words

4 Complete the text. Use the words in the box.

> arrived bus stop caught left stop
> ticket

I went to London last weekend. First, I
(1) …… a taxi to the train station. Then I
bought a **(2)** …… for the train. The train
(3) …… the station at 8.35. It was a very
fast train – it didn't **(4)** …… at any small
towns or villages. It **(5)** …… at Victoria
Station in London at 10.05. I waited for a
bus at the **(6)** …… next to Victoria Station.

In the home

5 Label the picture of the living room. Use the words in the box.

> armchair bookcase clock cupboard
> lamp mirror shelf sofa

Parts of a house

6 Copy and complete the names of the rooms. Use *a, e, i, o* and *u*.

1 b _ thr _ _ m   6 d _ n _ ng r _ _ m
2 b _ dr _ _ m   7 k _ tch _ n
3 st _ _ rs   8 g _ rd _ n
4 h _ ll   9 l _ v _ ng r _ _ m
5 t _ _ l _ t

GRAMMAR

Present tense contrast

1 Choose the correct verb form.

1 Dolphins **are eating** / **eat** fish.
2 **Is it raining** / **Does it rain** at the moment?
3 Look! John **is wearing** / **wears** my jacket.
4 She**'s always playing** / **always plays** volleyball on Fridays.
5 Angela isn't at home. She**'s visiting** / **visits** friends.
6 I**'m usually doing** / **usually do** my homework in my room.
7 We**'re going** / **go** swimming every Thursday.
8 Why **are you laughing** / **do you laugh**? What's funny?

Past simple affirmative

2 Write the past simple forms of these verbs. Are they regular or irregular?

1	work	4	chat	7	buy	9	get
2	study	5	meet	8	invite	10	tidy
3	eat	6	arrive				

Comparative and superlative adjectives

3 Complete the sentences. Use the comparative form of the adjectives.

1 Harry is generous, but Sarah is … .
2 Saturn is big, but Jupiter is … .
3 Gold is expensive, but diamonds are … .
4 I think Germany are good at football, but Brazil are ……. .
5 Dolphins are intelligent but chimps are … .
6 My bedroom is dirty, but your bedroom is … !

4 Complete the sentences. Use the superlative form of the adjectives in brackets.

1 Who is … girl in the class? (intelligent)
2 I think Los Roldan is … programme on TV. (good)
3 Which is … subject at school? (difficult)
4 Pele is one of … sportsmen in history. (famous)
5 David Bowie is …musician in Britain. (rich)
6 The River Plate is … river in the world. (wide)

should / shouldn't

5 Complete the sentences. Use *should*, affirmative or negative and the verbs in the box.

buy	drink	go out	smoke	study

1 'I'm thirsty'
  'You …… some water.'
2 'I think I'm going to fail my exams.'
  'You …… more.'
3 'I'm tired in the mornings.'
  'You …… every evening.'
4 'I love Maroon 5.'
  'You …… their new CD.'
5 'I've got a bad cough.'
  'You ……. .'

Past simple negative

6 Make these sentences negative.

1 We caught the train to Liverpool.
2 They arrived late.
3 She left home at eight o'clock.
4 You came to my party.
5 He played computer games last night.
6 I had pasta for dinner last night.

Past simple interrogative

7 Look at the chart. Write questions and short answers about Marta. Use the past simple.

Did Marta surf the Internet yesterday?
Yes, she did.

Yesterday ...

1	surf the Internet	✔
2	have a shower	✔
3	play basketball	✘
4	listen to music	✘
5	go to the cinema	✘
6	meet her friends	✔

Prepositions of movement

8 Look at the pictures and complete the text. Use the prepositions in the box.

across	down	over	through	under	up

He walked **(1)** ...... a bridge. Then he climbed **(2)** ...... a mountain and went **(3)** ...... a tunnel. He walked **(4)** ...... the mountain and swam **(5)** ...... a river. Finally he climbed **(6)** ...... a wall and arrived at the old castle.

Past continuous

9 Look at the pictures and complete the sentences with verbs from the box. Use the past continuous.

eat	watch	play	sit	talk	wear

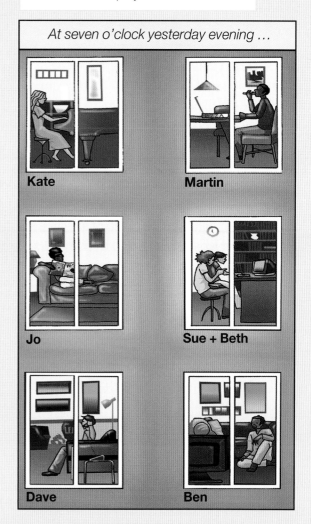

At seven o'clock yesterday evening ...

Kate   Martin

Jo   Sue + Beth

Dave   Ben

1 Kate ...... the piano.
2 Martin ...... a pizza.
3 Jo ...... on the sofa.
4 Sue and Beth ...... T-shirts.
5 Dave ...... on the phone.
6 Ben ...... TV.

10 Look at the picture again. Write questions and short answers. Use the past continuous.

1 Sue and Beth / play / a computer game
2 Martin / eat / a sandwich
3 Kate / wear / jeans
4 Ben / sit / sofa
5 Kate and Sue / chat
6 Jo / read / a magazine

1 Complete the text. Choose the correct words.

1 **a)** have   **b)** 'm having
2 **a)** across   **b)** through
3 **a)** visit   **b)** visited
4 **a)** go   **b)** went
5 **a)** better   **b)** more good
6 **a)** saw   **b)** seed
7 **a)** be   **b)** was
8 **a)** are singing   **b)** were singing
9 **a)** didn't play   **b)** not played
10 **a)** most exciting **b)** the most exciting
11 **a)** 'm loving   **b)** love
12 **a)** Did you have **b)** Had you

2 Answer the questions.

1 Where is Patricia?
2 What did she do last Saturday?
3 What is Patricia's opinion of the shops?
4 What were the man and women doing on the street?
5 What is Patricia's opinion of London?
6 Where did Julia go on holiday?

3 Correct the mistakes.

Maria is **most intelligent** girl in the class. ✗
Maria is the most intelligent girl in the class. ✓

1 He **didn't** wearing a jacket. ✗
2 What **you were doing** at six o'clock? ✗
3 You **should to** go to bed. ✗
4 He **doesn't should** copy your homework. ✗
5 New York is **more big** than London. ✗
6 She climbed **the mountain up**. ✗
7 Science is **interestinger** than maths. ✗
8 I **didn't met** my friends last night. ✗
9 **Does** he go out last night? ✗
10 It **doesn't rain** at the moment. ✗

Dear Julia,
I'm sending this postcard from London. I (1) ...... a fantastic time here on holiday with my cousins. Last Saturday we walked (2) ...... Tower Bridge, and then we (3) ...... the London Eye. Yesterday we (4) ...... shopping in the centre of the city. The shops here are (5) ...... than in Liverpool. We (6) ...... some great street musicians. A man (7) ...... playing the guitar and two women (8) .... We listened to them for ages. Unfortunately they (9) ...... any Robbie Williams songs! I think London is (10) ...... city in the world – I (11) ...... it! (12) ...... a good holiday in France? Write soon!
Love,
Patricia

3 Our world

WHAT'S IN THIS UNIT?

- The natural world
- Wildlife
- Countable and uncountable nouns
- *some* and *any*

- *How much / How many ... ?*
- Expressions of quantity
- Giving advice
- Preparing to write

VOCABULARY

The natural world

1 Match the words with the pictures. Then listen and repeat.

beach   island   lake   mountain   river   the sea   the sky   valley

2 Look at the photos. Complete the descriptions. Use the words in exercise 1.

I come from a small village in north Wales, Betws-y-Coed. It's in a deep (1) ...... between two tall (2) .... My house is next to a (3) .... You can see it in this photo. It's beautiful, but the water is very cold. There's also a (4) ...... near the village. We sometimes go swimming there in the summer.

I live in Torquay, in the south of England. This is a photo of a beach near the town. I often come here and swim in (5) .... There is one large (6) ...... about two kilometres from the beach. In this photo (7) ...... is really beautiful as the sun goes down.

More practice? ➤ **Workbook page 86** ➤

HARRY'S STORY

Climbing the wall

1 I really love the natural world. I like rock climbing but there aren't any mountains near here. Kelly likes rock climbing too. She went on a rock climbing holiday last year and saw an eagle! We decided to take Sarah to an indoor climbing centre to see if she liked it. She was very nervous.

It looks high! How many metres is it? I'm scared of heights – that's why I don't go rock climbing!

Kelly

Sarah

You shouldn't think about it too much.

2 Kelly and I didn't have any problems. But it was hard work! We got really hot and thirsty. I really wanted some water. Sarah was having a difficult time. Martin, the instructor helped her.

3 Later in the café it was good to have some food. There weren't any burgers or chips but I had a bar of chocolate. Sarah talked about Martin all the time.

Maybe I should come here again. It was hard and I didn't really enjoy it. But Martin was great!

Yes, you said that two minutes ago.

Keep going! You're nearly there. You shouldn't look down.

I can't move. I need some help!

1 🎧 Read and listen. Why does Sarah want to go rock climbing again? Choose the correct answer.

1 She thought it was easy.
2 She likes the climbing instructor.
3 She really enjoyed it.

2 Complete the sentences. Use the correct names.

1 … went on a rock climbing holiday last year.
2 … is scared of heights.
3 … wanted some water.
4 … couldn't move.
5 … helped Sarah.
6 … had a bar of chocolate.

3 REAL ENGLISH Who says these expressions? What do they mean?

1 I'm scared of heights.

2 But it was hard work!

3 Keep going.

4 It was hard.

Teen focus

Sports
Read what Kelly says about sport. What sports do you do and watch?

I really like sport. I play volleyball and do gymnastics at school. I like watching sport on TV too, especially football. I support Chelsea.

Word check Wildlife

4 Copy the chart. Look at the story and find the missing word.

land	air	water
tiger	_____	dolphin

5 Work in pairs. Add these words to the chart in exercise 4. How many more can you add?

whale   fly   shark   lion   bear   camel

More practice?	Workbook page 86

Study skills

Word stress

6 Say these words from the story. Put the stress on the underlined syllable.

natural   mountains   nervous
problems   instructor   chocolate

7 Which syllable is often stressed in English? Is it the same in your own language?

Countable and uncountable nouns

1 Look at the chart. Which group of nouns are countable and which group are uncountable?

Group 1
bread   homework   milk   water   money

Group 2
animal   beach   island   insect   photo

2 Add these nouns to the groups in exercise 1.

1 food   3 cheese   5 rice
2 whale   4 mountain   6 river

3 Copy and complete the table. Use *countable* and *uncountable*.

Rules	Examples
1 …… nouns usually have a singular and plural form.	a lake ✔ two lakes ✔
2 …… nouns only have a singular form.	milk ✔ milks ✘
3 We can only use *a/an* with singular …… nouns.	an insect ✔ a money ✘

4 Correct the mistakes.

I have breads for breakfast. ✘
I have bread for breakfast. ✔

1 Do you like a cheese? ✘
2 There's river near my house. ✘
3 I've got a lot of homeworks this weekend. ✘
4 I'm eating sandwich. ✘
5 Can I have a pasta, please? ✘

Pronunciation Intonation

5 🎧 Listen and repeat. Practise saying the sentences. Pay attention to the intonation.

Were there any lions?

There were some lions.

1 Have you got a cat?
  I haven't got a cat.
2 Did they see an elephant?
  They didn't see an elephant.

some and *any*

6 Read the *Take note!* box. Copy and complete the table with *some* and *any*.

> **Take note!**
>
> We use *some* in affirmative sentences.
> We use *any* in negative and interrogative sentences.

	Uncountable nouns	Countable nouns (plural)
Affirmative	There's **(1)** …… water.	There are **(4)** …… islands.
Negative	There isn't **(2)** …… water.	There aren't **(5)** …… islands.
Interrogative	Is there **(3)** …… water?	Are there **(6)** …… islands?

7 Complete the dialogue. Use *some* and *any*.

Tony I went to a safari park last weekend.
Nina Was it good?
Tony Yes, it was. There were **(1)** …… interesting animals.
Nina Were there **(2)** …… lions or tigers?
Tony There were **(3)** …… lions but there weren't **(4)** …… tigers. There was an elephant too. It was playing in **(5)** …… water.
Nina Did you take **(6)** …… photos?
Tony Yes, I did. I took **(7)** …… photos of the lions.
Nina Did you buy **(8)** …… souvenirs?
Tony No, I didn't. I didn't have **(9)** …… money!

| More practice? | Workbook pages 87–88 |

Dialogue

1 🎧 **Read and listen. Complete the dialogue with the words in the box.**

early   How   right   tired   today

GIVING ADVICE

Hannah Hi, Emily. (**1**) ...... are you?

Emily Not great.

Hannah Oh. What's the matter?

Emily I'm really (**2**) ...... and I've got a headache.

Hannah I don't think you should go out (**3**) .... I think you should go to bed (**4**) ....

Emily You're (**5**) ....

2 🎧 **Listen and repeat the phrases from the dialogue.**

1 Not great.
2 What's the matter?
3 I don't think you should go out.
4 I think you should go to bed early.

3 Practise reading the dialogue.

4 Write your own dialogue. Use the ideas in the box to help you or use your own.

Ideas for A	Ideas for B
exam tomorrow	not go to the party / do some revision
a bad leg	not play football / watch TV

A: Hi ... How ... ?
B: Not ...
A: Oh. What's ... ?
B: ...
A: I don't think ... I think ...
B: You're ...

5 Act out your dialogue.

Hi ... How ... ?

Not ...

More practice?   **Workbook page 89**

Listening

6 🎧 **Listen. What is Alex's problem? Choose the correct answer.**

a) He can't go to Kirstie's birthday party.
b) Kirstie is angry with him.
c) He hasn't got any money for Kirstie's present.

7 🎧 **Listen again. Choose the correct answers.**

1 Kirstie's birthday is on:
   a) Sunday   b) Saturday
2 Hannah thinks Alex should buy:
   a) a T-shirt   b) a CD
3 Kirstie's favourite singer is:
   a) Ricky Martin   b) Dido
4 Hannah thinks Alex should:
   a) make a CD   b) make a cake
5 They could make the cake at:
   a) Alex's house   b) Hannah's house

GRAMMAR 2

How much / How many ...?

1 Study the *Take note!* box. How do you say *How much* and *How many* in your language?

> ### Take note!
>
> We use *How much ...?* with uncountable nouns.
> **How much** money have you got?
> We use *How many ...?* with countable nouns.
> **How many** CDs have you got?

2 Complete the questions with *How much* or *How many*. Then guess the correct answer.

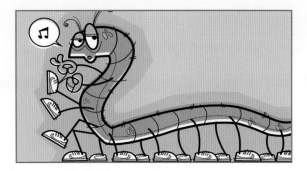

1 …… legs has a centipede got?
   a) about 30   **b)** about 100
   c) about 1,000.
2 …… new teeth does a tiger shark grow in ten years?
   a) about 240   **b)** about 2,400
   c) about 24,000.
3 …… water can a thirsty camel drink?
   a) about 13 litres **b)** about 30 litres
   c) about 130 litres.
4 …… centimetres can bamboo grow in a day?
   a) about 1cm   **b)** about 10cm
   c) about 90cm.
5 …… food does an elephant eat in one day?
   a) about 15 kilos **b)** about 150 kilos
   c) about 1,500 kilos.
6 …… hours a day does a koala bear sleep?
   a) about two   **b)** about nine
   c) about nineteen.

3 🎧 Listen and check your answers to exercise 2.

Expressions of quantity

4 Study the information.

> ### Take note!
>
> We can't use *a* or numbers with uncountable nouns. However, we can sometimes use other words with them when we want to talk about quantity.
> *I drank a glass of lemonade and I ate two pieces of cake.*

5 Match the words and pictures.

cake   milk   pasta   soup   sugar   water

1 a bowl of …   4 a piece of …
2 a glass of …   5 a bag of …
3 a bottle of …   6 a can of …

6 Complete the conversation. Use the words in the box.

bag   bottle   cans   cans   piece

Dad   I'm going to the supermarket. Do we need any food?

Mum Yes, could you get a (1) …… of rice, a (2) … of orange juice and two (3) … of tomato soup.

Dad   Anything else?

Mum Oh, yes. We need a large (4) … of Cheddar cheese and four (5) … of Coke.

Dad   OK.

More practice?   Workbook pages 87–88

Come to the West Coast of Scotland!

The West Coast of Scotland is a fantastic place for a holiday. There aren't any big cities, but there are lots of villages. There are beautiful lakes and rivers. There are also mountains – including Ben Nevis, the highest mountain in Britain.

One of the best places to visit is Inverawe Country Park. There are beautiful valleys and lakes and it's a great place for walking or cycling. You can see eagles and you can also go fishing in the lakes.

Another fantastic place is Ganavan Sands. It's one of the best beaches in Scotland. You can swim in the sea (but the water is cold!). You can sometimes see whales and dolphins in the sea near the beach.

Reading

1   Read the tourist leaflet. Find the name of a mountain, a park and a beach in the text.

2   Read the leaflet again. Answer the questions.

1   Are there any big cities in the region?
2   What is special about Ben Nevis?
3   Are there any valleys in Inverawe Country Park?
4   What kind of bird can you see in the park?
5   Where can you go fishing in the park?
6   What is the only problem with swimming in the sea?

3   **MAPS**   Find Ben Nevis, Ganavan and Inverawe on the map on page 66.

Writing   Preparing to write

> **Preparing to write**
>
> Make notes of your ideas before you begin to write. You don't need to write complete sentences.
> Mar del Plata: beautiful beaches – swimming, sunbathing
> Catedral Bariloche: mountains – skiing June to September

4   Choose a region of your country. Prepare to write a tourist leaflet about it. Make notes using these ideas.

name of region?	
big cities?	
Natural features: the sea? beaches? islands? mountains? rivers? lakes?	
activities?	
wildlife?	

5   Write a tourist leaflet like the one in exercise 1. Use the writing plan and your notes from exercise 4.

> Come to ... !
> **Paragraph 1**
> ... is a fantastic place ... There are ...
> **Paragraph 2**
> One of the best places to visit is ...
> There are ... It's a great place for ...
> You can see ...
> **Paragraph 3**
> Another fantastic place is ...
> There are ...   You can ...

More practice?	Workbook pages 89–90

FOCUS ON THE WORLD

1 🎧 Read the information. Find the name of:

a) the range of mountains where Everest is.
b) the oldest person to climb Everest.
c) the part of the mountain above 7,600 metres.

Everest

Everest is 8,850 metres high – the highest mountain in the world. It's in the Himalayas, in South Asia. Everest is between two countries, Nepal and Tibet.

Climbing Everest – quick facts

the first	Sir Edmund Hilary and Tenzing Norgay Sherpa in 1953
the youngest	Ming Kipa Sherpa (15-year-old girl) and Temba Chheri (15-year-old boy)
the oldest	Yuichiro Miura (70-year-old man)
the fastest	Pemba Dorje (in 12 hours 45 minutes)
the most times	Appa Sherpa (13 times so far)

Today, a lot of people are trying to climb Everest. They each pay about $65,000. There's a lot of rubbish on Everest now because climbers leave it there. The part of the mountain above 7,600 metres is called the 'Death Zone'. This is because there isn't much oxygen in the air, so it's difficult for climbers to breathe. They also get cold very fast and it's more difficult to think clearly. Most climbers take oxygen with them.

2 **MAPS** Find or mark Nepal and Tibet on the map on pages 68–9.

3 Complete the questions with the words in the box. Then write answers.

> How much   When   What   ~~Where~~   Who   Why

Where is Everest?
It's between Tibet and Nepal in South Asia.

1 ...... is there a lot of rubbish on Everest?
2 ...... were the first people to climb Everest?
3 ...... did the first people climb Everest?
4 ...... do climbers in the 'Death Zone' need?
5 ...... money do climbers pay to climb Everest today?

Song and Reading File page 57.

4 Going out

WHAT'S IN THIS UNIT?

- Places to go
- Food and drink
- *going to* and future time expressions

- *must / mustn't*
- In a café
- Using pronouns

VOCABULARY

Places to go

1 🎧 Match the words with the pictures. Then listen and repeat.

swimming pool   amusement arcade   aquarium   theme park
Internet café   museum   disco   restaurant

2 Use the chart to make sentences.

1 You can go on exciting rides at a theme park.

	Activities		Places
You can	go on exciting rides have dinner see very old things play video games send an email see sharks go swimming dance	at a/an	amusement arcade. swimming pool. Internet café. aquarium. museum. disco. theme park. restaurant.

3 In pairs, ask and answer about the places in exercise 1.

> How often do you go to a swimming pool?

> I often/sometimes/hardly ever/never go to a swimming pool.

| **More practice?** | **Workbook page 91** |

Don't judge by appearances

1 Last weekend there was a party in Harry's street. You know I love parties! There was lots of food. There were also games and competitions. Ali was there too. He goes to our school. He's from Morocco.

> Wow, look! I must try all the food here. What about you?

> I'm not going to try *everything*! I'm going to have a look around and decide.

Ali

Harry

2 We walked around and found Ali's mum's stall. Ali's family cooked some delicious Moroccan food. There were meat kebabs and salads. People were drinking special fruit juices and tea. Ali smiled when Harry put lots of sauce on his food.

> Are you going to tell us what this is?

> It's a special Moroccan sauce. I made it.

3 Harry thought it was tomato sauce. He was wrong. We laughed for a long time – Harry laughed too in the end!

> It's got forty-five hot chillies in it. Would you like some more?

> It isn't funny!

> It *is* funny! I'm going to remember this!

1 🎧 Read and listen. Why isn't Harry happy at the end?

1 Because the party is boring.
2 Because he doesn't like the food.
3 Because he chooses the wrong sauce.

2 Correct the false sentences.

1 There was a party in **Kelly's** street.
2 Ali comes from **Egypt**.
3 Kelly and Ali go to the same **church**.
4 Ali's **brother** had a food stall.
5 Harry thought the sauce was **chilli** sauce.
6 The sauce had **fifty-five** chillies in it.

3 **REAL ENGLISH** Who says these expressions? What do they mean?

> 1 What about you?

> 2 I'm going to have a look around.

> 3 In the end.

> 4 It isn't funny!

Word check Food and drink

4 Copy the chart. Add four more items from the story.

food	drink
apples	water
cheese	cola
bread	chocolate milkshake
(1) ……	(3) ……
(2) ……	(4) ……

More practice?	Workbook page 91

Study skills

Place names

5 Place names aren't always in dictionaries, but they're often different in different languages. Which of these place names are the same in your own language and which are different?

London   New York   Washington
Tokyo   Rome   Sydney   Cardiff
Edinburgh   Cape Town

Street parties
Read what Kelly says about street parties.
Do you have street parties or festivals where you live?

> The people in my street organise a street party every year in the summer. Everyone brings food and people dress up for it. It sometimes rains, but it's great fun.

GRAMMAR 1

going to and future time expressions

1 Copy and complete the table.

Affirmative	Negative
I' **(1)** ...... going to watch	I'm not going to watch
you're going to watch	you aren't going to watch
he's going to watch	he **(3)** ...... going to watch
she's going to watch	she isn't going to watch
it's going to watch	it isn't going to watch
we' **(2)** ...... going to watch	we aren't going to watch
you're going to watch	you aren't going to watch
they're going to watch	they **(4)** ...... going to watch

We use *going to* to talk about future plans and intentions.

2 Match the phrases (1–6) with the pictures (a–f). Write complete sentences with *going to* affirmative.

1 – c She's going to drink some milk.

1 drink some milk
2 see a film
3 cook a pizza
4 play computer games
5 watch a football match
6 spend the day at the beach

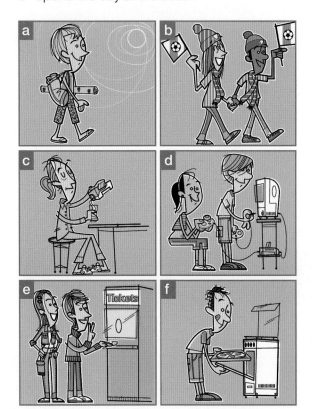

3 Complete the sentences. Use *going to* negative.

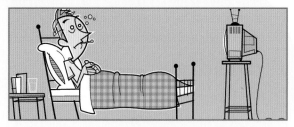

1 He ...... go to the amusement arcade because he's ill.

2 I ...... spend the afternoon at the theme park because it's raining.

3 We ...... meet at the swimming pool. We're going to meet at the Internet café.

4 My parents ...... come to cinema because they don't like science fiction films.

5 She ...... go to the party because she can't dance.

4 Put the future time expressions in the correct order.

Future time expressions
next month   tomorrow morning
~~this evening~~   next week   next year
tomorrow afternoon

this evening, ...

More practice?	Workbook pages 92–93

Pronunciation Contractions

5 🔊 Listen. Which sentence do you hear, a or b?

1 a) I could swim when I was three.
   b) I couldn't swim when I was three.

2 a) You should listen to him.
   b) You shouldn't listen to him.

3 a) We must use a computer.
   b) We mustn't use a computer.

Communicate!

Ask your partner four questions about what they are going to do in the summer holiday.

Are you going to stay with your uncle?

Dialogue

1 🎧 **Read and listen. Complete the dialogue with the words in the box.**

> six   milkshake   please   you   sandwich

IN A CAFÉ

MENU

Food
Salad £3.50
Baked potato and cheese £2.00
Sandwich (tomato, cheese, egg) £2.00
Pizza £2.50

Drinks
Cola £1.00
Orange juice £1.00
Milkshake £1.00
Tea £1.50

Waiter	Hi. Can I help you?
Emily	Yes. Can I have a tomato and cheese (**1**) ......, please?
Waiter	Sure. And for you?
Alex	A baked potato and cheese for me, (**2**) ....
Waiter	Anything to drink?
Emily	Can I have some cola, please?
Alex	And a (**3**) ...... for me, please.
Waiter	That's (**4**) ...... pounds, please.
Emily	Here you are.
Waiter	Thank (**5**) ....

2 🎧 **Listen and repeat the phrases from the dialogue.**

1 Can I help you?   3 Anything to drink?
2 And for you?   4 Here you are.

3 Practise reading the dialogue.

4 Write your own dialogue. Use the menu in exercise 1.

A: Hi. Can I help ... ?
B: Yes. Can I have ... ?
A: Sure. And for ... ?
C: A ...
A: Anything to ... ?
B: A ...
C: Can I have ... ?
A: That's ...
B: Here ...
A: Thank ...

5 In groups of three, act out your dialogue.

> Hi. Can I help ... ?

> Yes. Can I have ... ?

More practice?	Workbook page 94

Listening

6 🎧 Listen to Joe and Hannah ordering. What can't Joe have?

7 🎧 Listen again. Copy and complete the order.

Food
1 _____
2 _____

Drinks
1 _____
2 _____

Total: £ _____

GRAMMAR 2

going to interrogative

1 Copy and complete the table.

Interrogative
Am I going to watch?
(1) ...... you going to watch?
Is he going to watch?
Is she going to watch?
Is it going to watch?
(2) ...... we going to watch?
Are you going to watch?
Are they going to watch?

Short answers
Yes, I am. / No, I **(3)** ....
Yes, she **(4)** .... / No, she isn't.

2 Write questions and true answers. Use the interrogative of *going to*.

> you / travel / next year?
> *Are you going to travel next year?*
> *Yes, I am. / No, I'm not.*

1 you / visit a museum next week?
2 your friends / go swimming next Sunday?
3 you / go shopping next weekend?
4 you / do your homework this evening?

3 🎧 Complete the conversation. Use *going to* affirmative, negative and interrogative. Then listen and check.

Mark	What *are you going to do* (do) on Friday evening?
Dave	**(1)** ...... (go) to Jane's birthday party.
Mark	What **(2)** ...... you ...... (wear)?
Dave	Jeans and a T-shirt.
Mark	Who **(3)** ...... you ...... (go) with?
Dave	Kate and Sonia.
Mark	It's a long walk to Jane's house.
Dave	Oh, we **(4)** ...... (not walk). My dad **(5)** ...... (drive) us there. What about you? What **(6)** ...... you ......(do)?
Mark	I **(7)** ...... (go out) with Gloria. But we **(8)** ...... (not go) to Jane's party.
Dave	Why not?
Mark	She didn't invite us!

must / mustn't

4 Study the table. Is the third person (*he/she/it*) form different?

Affirmative
You must go.   She must go.   They must go.

Negative
I mustn't go.   He mustn't go.   We mustn't go.

5 Look at the rules for the computer game. Write sentences with *must* and *mustn't*.

Find the treasure.
> *You must find the treasure.*

1 Don't walk under the bridge.
2 Climb up the wall.
3 Don't open any red doors.
4 Don't drink or eat anything.
5 Run down the stairs.

More practice?   **Workbook pages 92–93**

Invitation to a birthday party

Hi Tania,

It's my birthday on Wednesday 24th. We've got school on that day, so I'm going to celebrate on Saturday. Are you free?

A lot of my friends are going to be there. In the afternoon, we're going to go to the cinema to see a film. It finishes at half past three. After that, we're going to prepare for the party. It's going to be a fancy dress party. The theme is 'horror'. I'm going to wear a monster costume. Sally is going to be a devil and I think Ben is going to be a ghost.

Danny's going to organise the music because he's got lots of great CDs. Jane and Freddy are going to go to the supermarket and buy some bread, cheese, pizzas, crisps and drinks. Then they're going to make some sandwiches and decorate the room. The party starts at seven.

I hope you can come.

Love, Chris

Reading

1 🎧 Read the email. What two things is Chris going to do to celebrate his birthday?

2 Read the text again. Answer the questions.

1 Why isn't Chris going to celebrate on Wednesday?
2 What are they going to see?
3 What type of party is it going to be?
4 Who's going to wear a devil costume?
5 Why is Danny going to organise the music?
6 What are Jane and Freddy going to buy?

Writing   Using pronouns

> **Take note!**
>
> We can use pronouns to avoid repeating names and nouns.
>
> We're going to go to the cinema to see a film. **It** finishes at half past three.
>
> **Danny** is going to organize the music because **he**'s got a lot of great CDs.

3 Replace the bold words with pronouns.

1 I love surfing. **Surfing** is exciting.
2 My sister loves computer games. She's very good at **computer games**.
3 Martin is my best friend. I often go to the amusement arcade with **Martin**.
4 My brother likes listening to music at discos but **my brother** doesn't like dancing.
5 My mum is 38. **My mum** is a nurse.

4 Imagine it's your birthday next week. Write an email about it to a friend.

> **Paragraph 1**
> Hi, ...
> It's my birthday ...
> **Paragraph 2**
> In the afternoon we're going to ...
> (Where? To do what? Who with?)
> **Paragraph 3**
> In the evening we're going to ...
> (Do what? Who with?)
> I hope you can come.
> Love, ...

| More practice? | Workbook pages 94–95 |

FOCUS ON THE WORLD

1 🎧 Read the texts and match them with the photos.

Food festivals

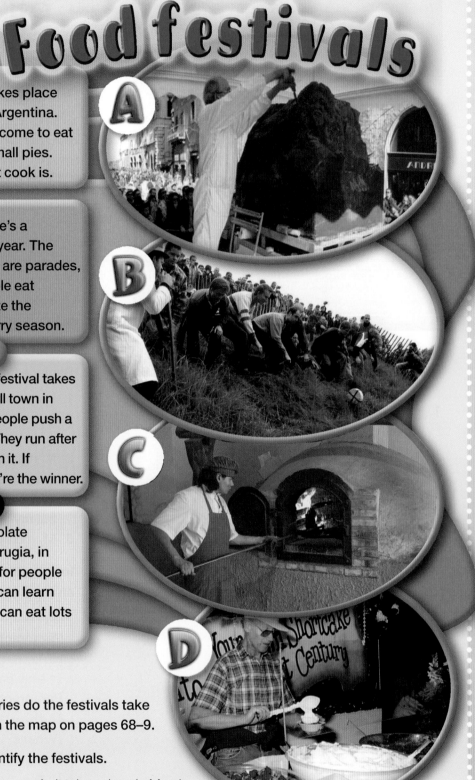

Empanada festival

1 The empanada festival takes place every year in Famaillá in Argentina. It's in September. People come to eat empanadas. These are small pies. They decide who the best cook is.

Strawberry festival

2 In Florida in the USA, there's a strawberry festival every year. The festival is in March. There are parades, games and funfairs. People eat strawberries and celebrate the beginning of the strawberry season.

Cheese-rolling festival

3 In May the cheese-rolling festival takes place in Gloucester, a small town in England. At the festival, people push a large cheese down a hill. They run after the cheese and try to catch it. If you catch the cheese, you're the winner.

Eurochocolate festival

4 In October, the Eurochocolate Festival takes place in Perugia, in Italy. This is a big festival for people who love chocolate. You can learn about chocolate and you can eat lots of chocolate too.

2 MAPS In which four countries do the festivals take place? Find or mark them on the map on pages 68–9.

3 Read the sentences and identify the festivals.

1 People run down a hill.
2 There are parades and funfairs.
3 It takes place in Italy.
4 It takes place in March.
5 It takes place in Argentina.
6 People choose the best cook.

Song and Reading File page 57.

5 The future

WHAT'S IN THIS UNIT?
- Computers
- Computer studies
- *will*
- First conditional
- At the cinema
- Using paragraphs

VOCABULARY

Computers

1 🎧 Match the words with the pictures. Then listen and repeat.

CD reader/writer disk keyboard mouse mouse mat printer
scanner screen speakers webcam base unit

2 Complete the definitions. Use words from exercise 1.

1 We use a …… to print information from a computer.
2 We use a …… to scan pictures into a computer.
3 We use a …… to record video pictures for a computer.
4 We use a …… to store information.
5 We use a …… to type information into a computer.
6 We use a …… to move around the screen.
7 We use …… to listen to music and sounds.

| More practice? | Workbook page 96 |

KELLY'S STORY

The Science of Sport

1 Last weekend Sarah and I went to the Science Museum in London. There's a great exhibition called, 'The Science of Sport'. It's really cool because you can try different sports. Computers scan your details and print a report of your performance. We met two boys there. They thought we couldn't do anything because we are girls. They were so annoying!

2 We ignored them, but they didn't go away. They asked us our names. Then, they invited us to go to a café. I had an idea.

We'll help if you want. You won't manage on your own.

If you give me the ball, I'll show you how to do it.

Let's have a go at this.

Why don't we have a race?

If you win, we'll go to the café with you.

OK!

Sarah

3 They were fast – but I was faster.

4 At first, they didn't believe the result. Fortunately, a webcam recorded all the races onto the computer, so we could watch it again. They couldn't argue with that! In the end, they left us alone.

I won!

She's right.

No you didn't. If you look at the screen you'll see.

1 🎧 **Read and listen. How does Kelly prove that she won the race?**

1 They watch a recording.
2 They run the race again.
3 They ask some other people.

2 **Answer the questions.**

1 Where did Sarah and Kelly go?
2 What can you do at the exhibition?
3 Why are the two boys they meet annoying?
4 Why do the girls decide to race the boys?
5 Who is the fastest?
6 What happens after the race?

3 **REAL ENGLISH** **Who says these expressions? What do they mean?**

1 Let's have a go at this.

2 We'll help if you want.

3 I had an idea.

4 She's right.

Teen focus

Technology
Read what Kelly says about technology.
What's your opinion?

I'm not really into technology. Computers, DVD players and things like that are useful, I suppose, but I'm not interested in how they work. A mobile phone is a the most useful piece of technology I've got. I use it every day.

Word check Computer studies

4 **In the story, find the verbs from these nouns.**

1 printer
2 scanner

5 **Match the verbs (1–6) with the nouns (a–f).**

1 – b type a text

1 type   a) a disk
2 visit   b) a text
3 eject   c) software
4 scan   d) a website
5 install   e) a CD
6 burn   f) a picture

| More practice? | Workbook page 96 |

Study skills

Using the Internet

6 You can use the Internet to improve your English and find information. Find a webpage about the Science Museum in London and answer these questions.

1 What road is it on?
2 What is the name of the café in the basement?
3 What is on at the Imax cinema?
4 What two kinds of shop can you find at the museum?

GRAMMAR 1

will

1 Study the table.

Affirmative	Negative	Interrogative
I'll buy	I won't buy	Will I buy?
you'll buy	you won't buy	Will you buy?
he'll buy	he won't buy	Will he buy?
she'll buy	she won't buy	Will she buy?
it'll buy	it won't buy	Will it buy?
we'll buy	we won't buy	Will we buy?
you'll buy	you won't buy	Will you buy?
they'll buy	they won't buy	Will they buy?
We use *will* to talk about predictions.	**Full forms** 'll = will won't = will not	**Short answers** Yes, I will. / No, I won't. Yes, she will. / No, she won't.

2 Complete the predictions about Richard's future. Use *'ll* or *won't*.

1 He ...... live in the USA.
2 He ...... live in England.
3 He ...... have any children.
4 He ...... be a teacher.
5 He ...... be a doctor.
6 He ...... go surfing.
7 He ...... have a dog.
8 He ...... have two cats.

3 Make your own predictions about life in the year 2050. Write sentences with *will* or *won't*.

all cars / be / electric
All cars will be electric.
1 people / live / on Mars
2 robots / do / all our housework
3 we / go / to school
4 the world / be / very polluted
5 computers / be / more intelligent than people
6 computers / be / smaller than a watch

4 Work in pairs. Write questions about your partner's future. Use *will*.

get married before you're 25?
Will you get married before you're 25?
1 pass your next English exam ?
2 be rich and famous ?
3 get a job ?
4 live in this town all your life ?
5 go to university ?
6 have a lot of children ?

5 Ask and answer the questions in exercise 4.

> Will you get married before you're 25?

> Yes, I will. / No, I won't.

Dialogue

1 🎧 Read and listen. Which ticket is for *Space Adventure*?

AT THE CINEMA

Woman	Can I help you?
Alex	Yes. I'd like two tickets for *Space Adventure*.
Woman	That's £7.60, please.
Alex	Here you are.
Woman	Thank you. Here's your change. The film starts in ten minutes. It's screen three.
Alex	OK. Thanks.
Emily	I'm going to buy some popcorn. Do you want anything to eat?
Alex	No, but I'll have something to drink.
Emily	OK. I'll buy a bottle of water.
Alex	Thanks. I'll wait here.

2 🎧 Listen and repeat the dialogue.

> **Take note!**
>
> We use *will* for talking about instant decisions.
> 'Do you want some cola or lemonade?'
> 'I'll have some cola, please.'
> Find three examples in the dialogue.

3 Write your own dialogue. Use a film that you like.

A: Can I ... ?
B: Yes. I'd ...
A: That's ... , please.
B: Here ...
A: Thank ... Here's ... The film ... It's ...
B: OK. ...
C: I'm ... Do you ... ?
B: No, but ...
C: OK. I'll ...
B: Thanks. I'll ...

4 Work in groups of three. Act out your dialogue.

Can I ... ?   Yes, I'd ...

More practice?	Workbook page 99

Listening

5 🎧 Listen to Hannah and her sister Kate. What kind of film do they buy tickets for?

a) an adventure film   **b)** a science fiction film
c) a comedy

6 🎧 Listen again. Choose the correct answer.

1 What kind of film is *Space Colony*?
   a) comedy   **b)** science fiction
2 How much are the tickets?
   a) £5 each   **b)** £10 each
3 Which screen is their film?
   a) four   **b)** six
4 What drink is Hannah going to buy?
   a) water   **b)** orange juice
5 What food does Kate want?
   a) a sandwich   **b)** a hamburger

GRAMMAR 2

will revision

1 Complete the interview with the scientist. Use *will* affirmative, negative or interrogative.

Interviewer What will life be like in 2050?
(**1**) …… it …… (be) very different?
Scientist Yes, it will. For example, cities
(**2**) …… (be) cleaner because
most people (**3**) …… (not drive)
cars. They (**4**) …… (ride) bicycles.
Interviewer What about homes?
Scientist All homes (**5**) …… (have)
computers. For example, you
(**6**) …… (not go) shopping for
food because your computer
(**7**) …… (buy) it on the Internet.

Communicate!

Make predictions about where your partner will be at these times: at 1 am, 9 am and 6 pm tomorrow, and at 2 pm on Saturday. Are they correct?

At 1 am you'll be in bed.

Pronunciation Stress and rhythm

2 🎧 Listen and repeat. Pay attention to the stress and rhythm.

1 They'll travel by bus.
2 We'll live near the sea.
3 We'll have a robot.
4 I'll work in a hospital.

First conditional

3 Study the *Take note!* box.

> **Take note!**
>
> We use the present simple in the *if* clause and the future with *will* in the main clause.
> If I **pass** my exams, I'**ll become** a scientist.

4 Match sentences (1–5) with sentences (a–e) and write the complete sentence.

1 – e If you finish your science project, your teacher will be happy.

1 If you finish your science project,
2 If the scanner doesn't work,
3 If you click on that icon,
4 If it's hot and sunny tomorrow,
5 If we haven't got any ink for the printer,

a) we'll take it back to the shop.
b) mum will buy some in town.
c) you won't need your jacket.
d) the disk will eject.
e) your teacher will be happy.

5 Complete the sentences. Use the present simple affirmative or negative.

1 If the shops …… (not be) open, I'll buy it on the Internet.
2 If he …… (visit) that website, he'll find information for his project.
3 If you …… (not hurry), you'll miss the bus.
4 If they …… (have) time, they'll help us to install the software.

6 Complete the sentences. Use the future with *will* affirmative or negative.

1 If you break that printer, I …… (not buy) a new one.
2 If I'm home before seven, I …… (send) you an email.
3 If you go to bed early, you …… (not be) tired in the morning.
4 If we go to London, we …… (buy) a new computer.

| More practice? | Workbook pages 97–98 |

Space Colony – A Better Home

A You'll live in a modern apartment with computers in every room. Each apartment will have a robot. The robot will cook all your food and clean the apartment every day.

B There won't be any cars in the space colony. When you arrive, we'll give everybody an electric skateboard. These will be safe and fast. There will also be electric buses.

C Children in the family won't go to school. They'll study maths, science and all the other subjects at home. Their teachers will be holograms. The children will learn quickly, so they won't have any homework.

D You'll find a lot of exciting things to do in your free time. If you like computer games, you'll love our Virtual Reality Amusement Arcade. You can travel to any place in the world or any time in history.

Reading

1 🎧 Read the advertisement. Match the paragraphs (A–D) with the headings (1–4).

1 Education   3 Home
2 Free time   4 Transport

2 Correct the sentences.

1 The apartments will be very old.
2 The domestic robot will cook but it won't clean.
3 There will be electric cars and buses in the space colony.
4 Children will only study maths and science.
5 They'll have homework every day.
6 There won't be anything to do in your free time.

Writing Using paragraphs

3 Match each sentence to one of the paragraphs in the advertisement (A–D).

1 If they ask a question, the hologram will tell them the answer.
2 There will be a bus stop in every street.
3 These computers will control the light and temperature in your apartment.
4 There will be Virtual Reality games for surfing and skiing.

4 Write an advertisement for a space colony. Use the writing plan to help you.

> Space colony – a better home
> **Paragraph 1: Home**
> You will live ...
> **Paragraph 2: Transport**
> There will be ...
> **Paragraph 3: Education**
> The children will ...
> **Paragraph 4: Free time**
> In your free time, you will ...

More practice?   **Workbook pages 99–100**

1 🎧 Complete the text. Use the adjectives in the box. Then listen and check your answers.

> big   hot   long   old   short

The Solar System

The Solar System is very **(1)** ...... – about five billion years. It's very **(2)** ...... too – its diameter is about twelve billion kilometres.

The Sun

The Sun is 150 million kilometres from Earth. It is very, very **(3)** ...... – about 16 million °C in the centre. Light from the Sun travels to the Earth in eight minutes and twenty seconds.

The planets

There are nine planets in the Solar System. The Earth goes around the Sun in 365 days – one year. On Mercury, a year is very **(4)** ...... – Mercury goes around the Sun in 88 days. On Pluto, a year is very **(5)** ...... because Pluto goes around the Sun in 245 earth years!

The moons

There are about 100 moons in the Solar System. They go around the planets. The Earth has got one moon but Mercury and Venus haven't got any moons. Jupiter has got 39 moons! One day, people will probably visit one of the moons of Jupiter.

> **Take note!**
>
> one billion = 1,000,000,000
> °C = degrees Celsius

2 Answer the questions.

1 How old is the Solar System?
2 How far is the Sun from the Earth?
3 How long does it take light from the Sun to reach the Earth?
4 How long is a year on Mercury?
5 How long is a year on Pluto?
6 How many moons has Jupiter got?

Song and Reading File page 57.

VOCABULARY

The natural world

1 Complete the sentences with the words in the box.

> beach   islands   lake   mountain   river
> sea   sky   valley

1 Dolphins live in the ....
2 At the ......, you can sit in the sun or go swimming in the sea.
3 Between two mountains, there's a ....
4 The Thames is a famous ...... in London.
5 Everest is the highest ...... in the world.
6 Titicaca is a ...... in Peru and Bolivia.
7 The Galapagos are ...... in Ecuador.
8 Early in the morning, the ...... is often red.

Wildlife

2 Put the animals in the correct group.

> bull   eagle   fly   lion   insect
> shark   tiger   whale

No legs	Two legs	Four legs	Six legs+

Places to go

3 Complete the sentences with the words in the box.

> amusement arcade   aquarium   party
> Internet café   museum   theme park

1 We're going on an exciting ride. We're at a ....
2 We're looking at sharks and dolphins. We're at an ....
3 I'm drinking some cola and sending an email. I'm at an ....
4 We're playing video games. We're at an ....
5 I'm looking at some very old and interesting things. I'm at a ....
6 We're dancing to some fantastic music. We're at a ....

Food and drink

4 Complete the names of the food and drink.

Food

 1 c ......

 2 s ......

 3 a ......

 4 c ......

Drink

 1 o ...... j ......

 2 l ......

 3 w ......

 4 h ...... c ......

Computers

5 Put the letters in the correct order.

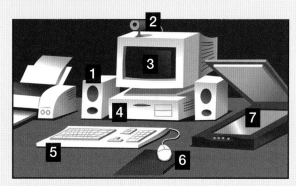

tiprnre printer

1 rekasep
2 bacmew
3 recnes

4 sabe nuti
5 dreybako
6 umsoe
7 recsnan

Computer studies

6 Complete the sentences.

> CD   disk   picture   software   text
> website

1 She's installing some new ....
2 I'm typing some ....
3 They're burning a ....
4 I'm visiting a ....
5 He's scanning a ....
6 I'm ejecting the ....

GRAMMAR

Countable and uncountable nouns

1 Find the eight uncountable nouns.

> beach   milk   island   book   homework
> shop   money   water   tiger   rice   mouse
> cheese   bread   carrot   apple   food

some and *any*

2 Choose *some* or *any*.

Paul and Ben are going camping.

Paul It's time to go. Are we ready?

Ben Yes, we are … I think. Here are my bags.

Paul What about food? Have we got (**1** some / any) rice?

Ben Yes, we have. We've got (**2** some / any) eggs and (**3** some / any) cheese too, but we haven't got (**4** some / any) bread.

Paul Have we got (**5** some / any) biscuits?

Ben Yes, we have. Oh no! We haven't got (**6** some / any) crisps.

Paul Well, that doesn't matter. Let's go!

How much / How many …?

3 Complete the questions with *How much* or *How many*. Then look at the picture and answer the questions.

How much cheese have they got?
They've got 1 kilo.

1 …… …… eggs have they got?
2 …… …… water have they got?
3 …… …… milk have they got?
4 …… …… potatoes have they got?
5 …… …… rice have they got?

Expressions of quantity

4 Complete the sentences with an expression of quantity.

> a glass of   a can of   a piece of
> a bowl of   a bottle of   a bag of

1 I usually have …… cereal for breakfast.
2 My aunt loves …… cake with her tea.
3 Can you buy …… flour at the shops?
4 You should take …… water with you to the gym.
5 To make spaghetti Bolognese you need …… tomatoes.
6 Mmm. I'd love …… fruit juice.

going to and future time expressions

5 Find the six future time expressions.

> today   tomorrow   next month   yesterday
> next week   last Monday   this evening
> tomorrow morning   next year   last June

6 Complete the dialogue. Use *going to* affirmative, negative and interrogative.

Lucy What (**1**) …… you …… (do) this weekend?

Brad I (**2**) …… (study). I've got exams next week!

Lucy I know, but it's Vicky's birthday on Saturday. She (**3**) …… (have) a party.

Brad (**4**) …… you …… (go)?

Lucy Yes, of course. She's my best friend.

Brad I (**5**) …… (not go). I like Vicky, but I don't like her brothers.

Lucy Her brothers (**6**) …… (not be) there. They (**7**) …… (be) at a different party.

Brad Really? That's great! See you at the party.

Lucy When (**8**) …… you …… (study)?

Brad On Sunday!

must / mustn't

7 Look at the signs. Write sentences with *You must …* or *You mustn't …*.

| 1 swim | 3 take photos |
| 2 run | 4 be silent |

will

8 Look at the pictures of Sonia's future. Complete the text with *'ll* or *won't*.

She (**1**) …… be a teacher. She (**2**) …… teach maths. She (**3**) …… have a husband called Mark. He (**4**) …… have fair hair. He (**5**) …… have dark hair. They (**6**) …… have two children. They (**7**) …… live in a big city. They (**8**) …… live in the mountains.

9 Write questions and short answers about Sonia's future. Use the correct form of *will*.

1 Sonia / be / a doctor
2 Sonia / be / a teacher
3 Sonia / teach / history
4 Sonia / have / a husband
5 Sonia's husband / have / dark hair
6 they / live / in a big city

First conditional

10 Complete the sentences with the verbs in the box. Use the present simple, affirmative or negative.

| rain   not study   visit   want   win |

1 If she …… , she won't pass the exam.
2 If my favourite team …… , I'll be very happy.
3 If you …… my website, you'll find some interesting information.
4 If he …… a sandwich, he'll go to the shop.
5 If it …… tomorrow, we won't play tennis.

11 Complete the sentences with the verbs in the box. Use the future with *will* affirmative or negative.

| be   not be   go   not know   send |

1 If it's sunny this afternoon, we …… to the beach.
2 If you don't phone her, she …… about the party.
3 If she has a big lunch, she …… hungry this afternoon.
4 If I find an Internet café, I …… you an email.
5 If we don't finish our project, the teacher …… angry.

BUILD UP (Units 1-5) ▷▷

1 Complete the email. Choose the correct words.

1 a) willn't   b) won't
2 a) had   b) haved
3 a) danced   b) dance
4 a) there was   b) there's
5 a) cry   b) crying
6 a) make   b) 'm making
7 a) biggest   b) bigest
8 a) I   b) I'll
9 a) some   b) any
10 a) you going   b) are you going
11 a) 'll be   b) 're
12 a) must to   b) must

2 Complete the questions for these answers.

When does the school year finish?
Tomorrow.
1 When ...... Patricia ...... exams for singing and dancing?
Last week.
2 What ...... her mum ...... at the concert?
She was crying.
3 Where ...... Patricia ...... in July and August?
In London.
4 Who ...... Patricia some money?
Her mum.
5 What ....?
It's nearly 12 o'clock.

3 Correct the mistakes.

He **do** his homework every evening. ✗
He does his homework every evening. ✔
1 I **not like** cheese. ✗
2 **Are wearing you** a jacket? ✗
3 He **can't to sing**. ✗
4 My bike is **more new** than your bike. ✗
5 **He's tallest** boy in the class. ✗
6 I **meeted** my friends at the beach. ✗
7 She **were listening** to music. ✗
8 Are you **going watch** a video tonight. ✗
9 **How many** bread is there? ✗
10 You **no must run** in the classroom. ✗
11 The weather **will to be** sunny tomorrow. ✗
12 If we go shopping tomorrow, **we buy** a new printer. ✗

Dear Julia,
School finishes tomorrow. It will be my last day at the School of Performing Arts. It's really sad. After the weekend, I (1) ...... see this bedroom again!
Last week, we (2) ...... exams for singing and dancing. I didn't (3) ...... very well, but the singing was OK. On Saturday evening, (4) ...... a concert for all the students' friends and families. Mum and Dad were there. I could see Mum when I was singing. She was (5) ......! Maybe she didn't like the song.
I'll be in London in July and August. I (6) ...... a CD of my songs. I'm going to take it to the (7) ...... record companies in London. If they like it, (8) ...... be a pop star! London's expensive, but Mum's going to give me (9) ...... money. What (10) ...... to do in the summer? If you (11) ...... going to be in London, let's meet up.
I (12) ...... go to bed now. It's nearly midnight. Hope to see you soon.
Love,
Patricia

SONG AND READING FILE

Justin Timberlake

Toploader

Emma Bunton

Atomic Kitten

Youngest Everest!

Bethany surfs again!

A question of taste

What's the big idea?

Cry me a river

1 🎧 **Listen and complete the song with the words in the box.**

did you leave   didn't know   didn't think   found out   told

You were my sun,
You were my earth,
But you (**1**) ...... all the ways I loved you, no.
So you took a chance
And made other plans,
But I bet you (**2**) ...... that they would come
    crashing down, no.

You don't have to say what you did,
I already know, I (**3**) ...... from him.
Now there's just no chance for you and
    me, there'll never be.
And don't it make you sad about it?

You told me you loved me –
Why (**4**) ...... me all alone?
Now you tell me you need me
When you call me on the phone.
Girl, I refuse – you must have me confused
With some other guy.
Your bridges were burned, and now it's
    your turn
To cry, cry me a river
Cry me a river,
Cry me a river,
Cry me a river, yeah, yeah.

> **I bet** = I'm sure
> **guy** = man, boy
> **don't it** = doesn't it

I know that they say
That some things are better left unsaid.
It wasn't like you only talked to him, and
    you know it.
(Don't act like you don't know it.)
All of these things people (**5**) .... me
Keep messing with my head
(Messing with my head).
You should have picked honesty,
Then you may not have blown it.

2 **Match the phrases (1–4) with the meanings (a–d).**

1   your bridges were burned
2   act like
3   messing with my head
4   blow it

a)   pretend (that)
b)   miss a good chance; fail to take an
      opportunity
c)   it was impossible to go back
d)   making me confused and unhappy

3 **Read the Songfile. Correct the sentences.**

1   The song is from *N Sync's* CD *Justified*.
2   The song reached number 1 in the UK
     charts.
3   Justin Timberlake was born in 1971.
4   He is Britney Spears' boyfriend.
5   He's still a member of the band *N Sync*.

Songfile

Song facts The song is from Justin Timberlake's CD *Justified*. It reached number 2 in the UK charts in 2003. The song was originally a hit for Julie London in 1957.

Artist facts Justin Timberlake was born on 31st January 1981 in Memphis, Tennessee. He appeared on the TV show *The New Mickey Mouse Club*, with Britney Spears. He became her boyfriend, but they split up in 2002. In 1997 he joined the group *N Sync*, but he left in 2002 and is now a solo artist.

Website www.justintimberlake.com

Dancing in the moonlight

1 🎧 Listen and complete the song with the adjectives in the box.

natural   fine   big   supernatural   warm

We get it on most every night
When that moon is (**1**) ...... and bright.
It's a supernatural delight.
Everybody was dancing in the moonlight.

Everybody here is out of sight.
They don't bark and they don't bite.
They keep things loose, they keep it tight.
Everybody was dancing in the moonlight.

Dancing in the moonlight.
Everybody was feeling (**2**) ...... and bright.
It's such a fine and (**3**) ...... sight.
Everybody was dancing in the moonlight.

We like our fun and we never fight.
You can't dance and stay uptight.
It's a (**4**) ...... delight.
Everybody was dancing in the moonlight.

Dancing in the moonlight.
Everybody was feeling warm and bright.
It's such a (**5**) ...... and natural sight.
Everybody was dancing in the moonlight.

we get it on = we dance
most every = almost every
out of sight = amazing
keep things loose = relax

2 Choose the best adjective to describe the feeling of the song.

a) bored   b) sad   c) happy

3 Read the Songfile. Are the sentences true or false? Correct the false ones.

1   There are six members in the band.
2   There are two guitarists in the band.
3   The band are all from the same town.
4   *Dancing in the moonlight* is from their second album.
5   *Magic Hotel* reached number one in 2000.

Songfile

Song: *Dancing in the moonlight*   **Band:** Toploader

Song facts : This was their first song and it reached number 7 in the UK chart in November 2000. It's from their first album, *Onka's Big Moka.*

Band facts : **Members:** Joseph (singer, keyboard), Julian (guitar), Dan (guitar), Matt (bass), and Rob (drums).
Nationality: English (They're from Eastbourne, a town on the south coast of England).
Albums: *Onka's Big Moka* reached number 4 in the UK chart in June 2000, and *Magic Hotel* reached number 3 in August 2002.

3 Sunshine on a rainy day

1 🎧 **Listen and complete the song with the words in the box.**

> desert   night   ocean   sea   skies   sunshine

Emma Bunton

2 **Find three 'weather' words in the song.**

1 r ......   2 s ......   3 w ......

3 **Read the Songfile. Answer the questions.**

1   Which CD is the song on?
2   Who originally sang it?
3   Where is Emma Bunton from?
4   Which band did she join in 1996?
5   When did the band split up?

Yeah, yeah.
Ooh, ooh-ooh.

I see you in the darkness.
I see you in the light.
I see your eyes shining
In through the (1) ....

Make me feel, make me feel
Like I belong.
Don't relieve me, you won't leave me here
All alone.

Cast your eyes
Like summer (2) ....
Blue earth and the (3) ....
Clearer than the skies, yeah!

Sunshine on a rainy day (sunshine)
Makes my soul, makes my soul drip, drip,
  drip away.
Sunshine on a rainy day (sunshine)
Makes my soul, makes my soul drip, drip,
  drip away.

You touch me with your spirit,
You touch me with your heart,
You touch me in the darkness,
I feel it start.

Make it feel, make it feel
So unreal (so unreal),
Like a wind in the (4) ...... ,
Like a moon on the (5) ....

Sunshine on a rainy day (sunshine)
Makes my soul, makes my soul drip, drip,
  drip away.
Sunshine on a rainy day (sunshine)
Makes my soul, makes my soul drip, drip,
  drip away.

Songfile

Song facts Emma Bunton's version of the song is on the CD *A Girl Like Me* (2001). The original song is by Zoe (1991).

Singer profile Emma Bunton was born on 21st January 1976 in London. She went to drama school. In 1996 she joined the *Spice Girls*. Her nickname was 'Baby Spice'. The band had nine number 1 hits and became one of the most successful girl bands in history. The *Spice Girls* split up in 1999 and Emma started a solo career.

Website www.emmabuntonofficial.com

The tide is high

1 Listen and complete the song with the words in the box.

believe   girl   gives up   know   tease   wait

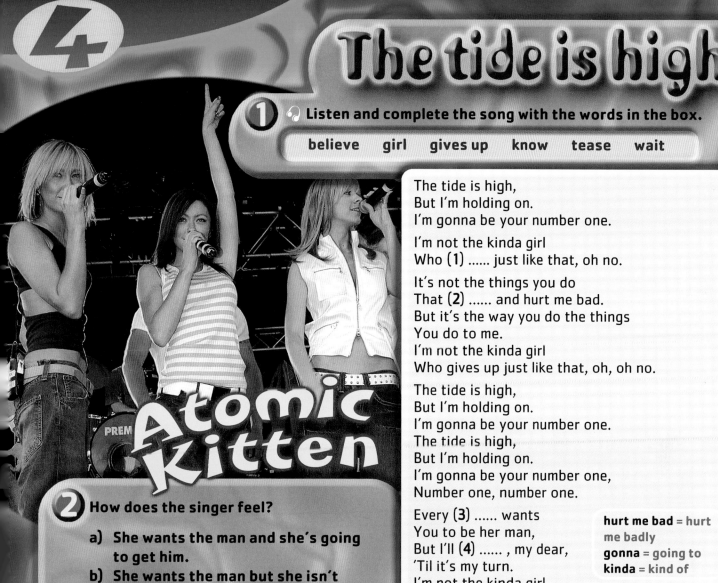

Atomic Kitten

The tide is high,
But I'm holding on.
I'm gonna be your number one.

I'm not the kinda girl
Who (1) ...... just like that, oh no.

It's not the things you do
That (2) ...... and hurt me bad.
But it's the way you do the things
You do to me.
I'm not the kinda girl
Who gives up just like that, oh, oh no.

The tide is high,
But I'm holding on.
I'm gonna be your number one.
The tide is high,
But I'm holding on.
I'm gonna be your number one,
Number one, number one.

Every (3) ...... wants
You to be her man,
But I'll (4) ...... , my dear,
'Til it's my turn.
I'm not the kinda girl
Who gives up just like that, oh no.

> **hurt me bad** = hurt me badly
> **gonna** = going to
> **kinda** = kind of

Every time that I get the feeling,
You give me something to believe in.
Every time that I've got you near me,
I don't (5) ...... that I want it to be.
But you know that I'm gonna take my chance now.
I'm gonna make it happen somehow.
And you (6) ...... I can take the pressure,
A moment's pain for a lifetime of pleasure.

Every girl wants you to be her man,
But I'll wait right here
'Til it's my turn.
I'm not the kinda girl
Who gives up just like that, oh no.

2 How does the singer feel?

a) She wants the man and she's going to get him.
b) She wants the man but she isn't going to get him.
c) She's going to get the man but she doesn't want him.

3 Read the Songfile. Answer the questions.

1 Who had a hit with the song in 1980?
2 When did *Atomic Kitten* have a hit with it?
3 Which original member left the band in 2001?
4 What was the group's most successful song?
5 When did *Atomic Kitten* split up?

Songfile

Song *The tide is high (Get the feeling)*   **Group** Atomic Kitten

Song facts : 1965 – original version by *The Paragons*. 1980 – UK number 1 for *Blondie* 2002 – UK number 1 for *Atomic Kitten*

Group facts : The three members were Tash, Liz and Jen. Jen joined in 2001 when original member Kerry left to have a baby with Bryan McFadden from the group *Westlife*. Their biggest hit was their fifth single, *Whole again*. It was number 1 in 2001 the UK and in many other countries. The band split up in 2004.

Read More!

1 Look at the photo. How old do you think the boy is? Read the text quickly and check your idea.

2 Read the text again. Put the events in the correct order.

- ☐ Temba took off his gloves.
- ☐ Temba reached the top of Mount Everest.
- ☐ 1 Temba started to climb with his brother and father.
- ☐ Some people were very angry.
- ☐ Temba thought, 'Now I'm going back to school.'
- ☐ The weather became terrible.
- ☐ Temba left school again.
- ☐ Temba went to hospital.

3 Are the sentences true or false? Correct the false ones.

Temba wanted to climb K2.
Temba didn't want to climb K2. He wanted to climb Mount Everest.

1 Temba climbed the mountain with his mother.
2 In May 2000 they started the first part of the journey.
3 At the top of the mountain the weather was terrible.
4 Temba lost six fingers.
5 He reached the top on 24th June.
6 At the top he thought about his friends and family.

4 Do you think Temba was too young to climb Everest? Why? / Why not?

Profile: Youngest Everest!

Temba Tsheri comes from Nepal. He looks like an ordinary schoolboy, but he had a dream: he wanted to climb Mount Everest.

In March 2000 he started to climb with his father and his brother. He was only fourteen years old. It was a very slow and dangerous journey. They struggled in strong wind and deep snow. On 21st May 2000 they started the final part of the journey. They were tired and cold and they didn't have much food.

When they were only 50 metres from the top, the weather suddenly became terrible. Then Temba stopped to tie his boots. He took off his gloves and his hands got frostbite. He hurried down the mountain and went to hospital. But it was too late. He lost five fingers.

After that, some people were very angry. They didn't want children on a dangerous mountain. But Temba wanted to try again. So, in April 2001, Temba left his school again. His school friends and teachers clapped and cheered, and gave him money for the climb. This time he didn't fail. He reached the top of the mountain on 23rd May.

He was just 16 years old – the first schoolboy to climb Mount Everest and the youngest person to do so.

What did Temba think when he reached the top? 'It was a great view. I remembered my friends and family. It was quite a difficult climb. It was cold and tiring but I didn't lose hope. And I succeeded! Now I'm going back to school.'

The Nepalese government gave Temba a Youth Excellence Award on 31 May 2001 which included a gold medal.

1 Look at the photo of Bethany Hamilton. How old is she, do you think? What's she doing?

2 Read the newspaper article.

Bethany surfs again!

In January 2004 thirteen–year–old Bethany Hamilton came fifth in a major surfing competition. Everyone was amazed. Not because she was so young, but because she's got only one arm.

Bethany lost her left arm in a terrible accident. On 31 October 2003, the sun was shining, and it was a perfect day for surfing. Bethany was lying on her surfboard about 300 metres from the beach in Hawaii. She was waiting for a big wave. Suddenly something pulled at her arm in the water. Under her surfboard was a huge tiger shark with her arm in its mouth. The sea was red with blood. It all happened so fast that she didn't even scream. Her friends helped her back to the beach. She was very shocked, and worried that she could never surf again. But four weeks after the accident she was surfing again! 'I was so happy, I cried,' she said. Bethany is writing a book about her experience. But her big ambition is to be a professional surfer. Before her accident she came second in the American Under–18 National Surfing Competition. Next time she wants to come first.

3 Read the text again. Find the answers to these questions.

1 Why was everyone amazed when Bethany came fifth in a surfing competition?
2 When was the accident?
3 Where did the accident happen?
4 Why didn't she scream when the shark attacked her?
5 When did she start to surf again?
6 What's she doing now?
7 What does she want to do in the future?

4 Work in pairs. Roleplay an interview with Bethany. Student A: prepare questions using the prompts. Student B: prepare the answers

1 what / weather / like / 31st October 2003
2 what / you / doing / when / shark/ attack
3 how / you / feel
4 what / your friends / do?
5 how important / surfing / in your life / now?

1 Look at the photos of the food. Would you like to try any of the dishes?

2 Read the text. Where are these foods eaten?

1 bird's nest soup China   4 fried spiders
2 1000-year-old eggs   5 fried ants
3 tarantulas   6 witchetty grubs

A question of taste

Every country in the world has its own food. Some dishes seem strange to us – but remember, some of our dishes seem strange to them!

Bird's nest soup is a delicacy in many Asian countries, especially China. They collect the nests from the caves where the birds live. The birds make the nests from saliva, and this gives the soup its special flavour. There is also a Chinese dish called 'thousand-year-old-eggs'. In fact, the eggs are only about a hundred *days* old – but that's old for an egg! The white part of the egg becomes dark, and the yellow part becomes green.

Many people are frightened of spiders, but the Piaroa Indians of Central America love tarantulas. They cook the spiders over a fire and then eat them. The most delicious parts are the big, hairy legs, they say. In Cambodia, you can buy fried spiders in the street and eat them as a snack.

In Europe people don't eat insects very often, but they're popular in many other countries. For example, fried ants are a popular snack in parts of Colombia. (They taste like bacon.) Witchetty grubs are a traditional food of the Australian Aborigines, and now you can eat them in lots of restaurants in Australia.

Like everything in the world, food is becoming more global. For example, cheese was never popular in China or Japan, but every year the Chinese and Japanese buy more and more cheese. Maybe one day, spiders and insects will be popular dishes in your country!

3 Read the text. Answer the questions.

1 In bird's nest soup, what are the nests made from?
2 How old are thousand-year-old eggs?
3 Which are 'the most delicious parts' of the tarantula?
4 In Cambodia, where do they sell fried spiders?
5 What do fried ants taste like?
6 Who traditionally eats witchetty grubs?

Word check

4 Find the words and phrases (1–4) in the text. Then match them with the meanings (a–d).

1 delicacy   a) the taste of food
2 cave   b) a small, quick meal
3 flavour   c) a big hole under the ground
4 snack   d) delicious food

Read More!

What's the big idea?

When people try to make predictions about the future, they usually get them completely wrong. For example, T.J. Watson, the head of IBM Computers, said in 1943: 'I think there may be a world market for five computers in total.' Today, people buy about 45 million PCs in the USA alone. Nanotechnology is the science of building tiny machines, so small that you cannot see them. Most scientists agree that nanotechnology will change our lives in the future – but how? It's difficult to predict whether this new technology will be like a wonderful dream, or a terrible nightmare.

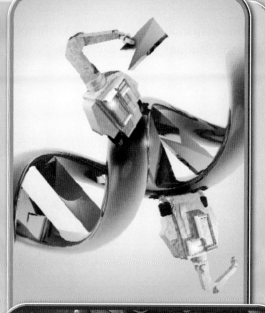

The Dream

Scientists are already making nanobots – tiny robots that are smaller than a virus. In the future, doctors will inject these into a patient, and the nanobots will travel around the body and repair any damage. They'll be able to cure almost every disease. There will be nanobots that can destroy cancer cells, nanobots that can cure diseases like AIDS, nanobots that can repair your heart or lungs.

The Nightmare

Some people are worried that nanotechnology will be difficult to control. Nanobots might escape and cause damage to people, plants and animals. Other people are worried that nanobots will be able to make copies of themselves using the materials around them – and this is where the nightmare begins. In Michael Crichton's book *Prey*, nanobots make copies of themselves so quickly that they use all the materials around and then look for more … and more, and more, eventually 'eating' the world. Some scientists think that this might really happen.

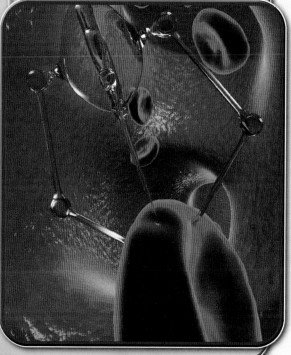

1 Read the text quickly. Which two sentences are true?

1 Nanobots are tiny robots.
2 Nanobots are tiny animals.
3 Nanobots are too small to see.
4 Nanobots already exist.
5 In the future, scientists will be able to cure diseases by injecting nanobots into patients.
6 Michael Crichton invented nanobots.
7 Some scientists are worried that nanobots could 'eat' the world.

2 Read the text. Are these sentences true or false?

1 T.J. Watson was correct about the future of the PC.
2 Most scientists think that nanotechnology with be important in the future.
3 It's easy to predict how nanotechnology will affect our lives.

3 Give examples of how:

1 technology is making life better.
2 technology is making life worse.

4 Class vote. How many students agree with this statement? How many disagree?

'Technology is making the world better.'

The British Isles

This map includes all the cities referred to in the Student's Book exercises.

Scotland

Ben Nevis
Ganavan
Inverawe

United Kingdom

Edinburgh

Northern Ireland
Belfast

Isle of Man

Republic of Ireland

Dublin

Bolton
Liverpool
Manchester
Betws-y-Coed

England

Wales

Stratford-Upon-Avon

Gloucester
Luton

Cardiff

Reading
London

Glastonbury
Hastings

Torquay

0   100 km

Channel Islands

Europe

Iceland

North
Atlantic
Ocean

Sweden

Finland

Norway

Estonia

Latvia

Denmark

Lithuania

Belarus

Northern
Ireland

Republic
of Ireland

United
Kingdom

Netherlands

Poland

Ukraine

Belgium

Germany

Czech
Republic

Moldova

Canary Islands

Luxembourg

Slovakia

France

Austria

Hungary

Romania

Switzerland

Slovenia

Croatia

Yugoslavia

Bosnia

Bulgaria

Italy

Macedonia

Portugal

Spain

Albania

Greece

Turkey

Mediterranean Sea

The World

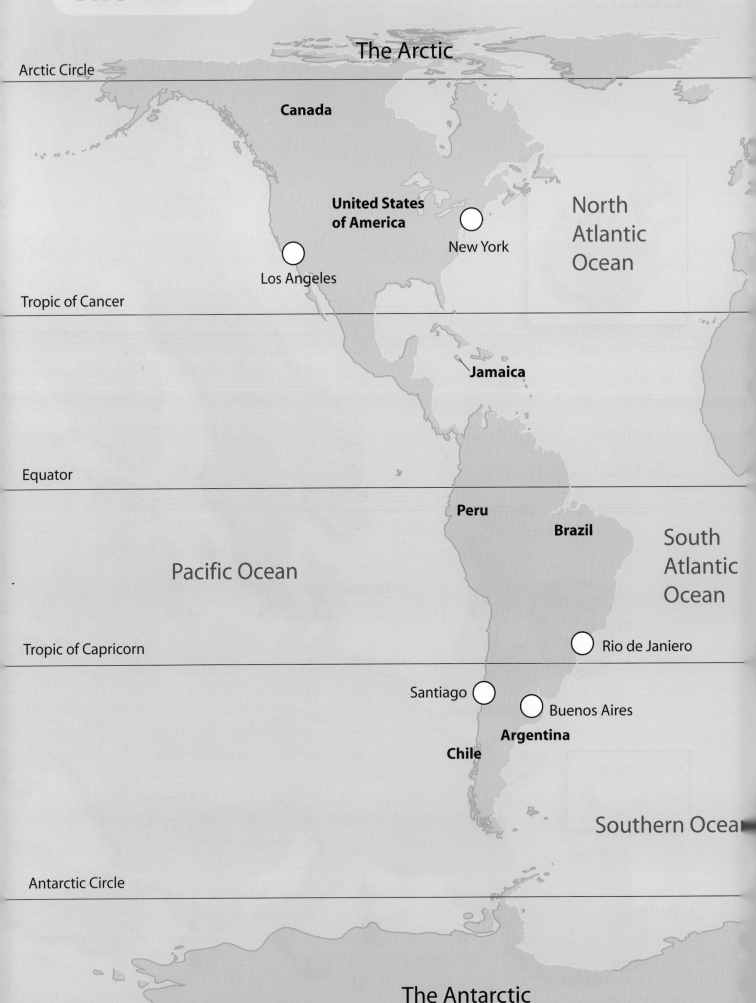

The Arctic

Arctic Circle

Canada

United States
of America

New York

North
Atlantic
Ocean

Los Angeles

Tropic of Cancer

Jamaica

Equator

Peru

Brazil

South
Atlantic
Ocean

Pacific Ocean

Tropic of Capricorn

Rio de Janiero

Santiago

Buenos Aires

Argentina

Chile

Southern Ocean

Antarctic Circle

The Antarctic

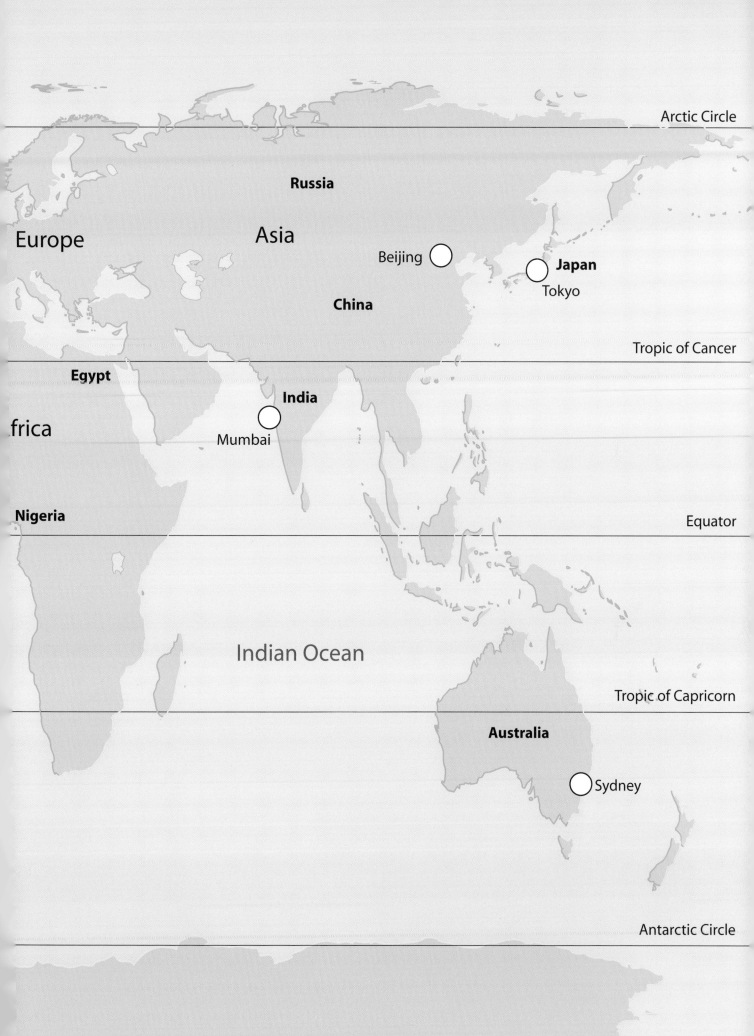

Arctic Circle

Russia

Europe

Asia

Beijing

Japan

Tokyo

China

Tropic of Cancer

Egypt

India

frica

Mumbai

Nigeria

Equator

Indian Ocean

Tropic of Capricorn

Australia

Sydney

Antarctic Circle

OXFORD

WORKBOOK

Introduction

VOCABULARY

→ Student's Book page 4

Revision: clothes

1 Complete the words. Use *a*, *e*, *i*, *o* and *u*.

1 j _ ck _ t
2 c _ p
3 tr _ _ n _ rs
4 tr _ cks _ _ t
5 sw _ _ tsh _ rt
6 j _ _ ns
7 sk _ rt
8 tr _ _ s _ rs
9 dr _ ss
10 s _ cks

Revision: activities

2 Complete the sentences. Use the present continuous. Then match them to the pictures.

1 He ...... a magazine.
2 He ...... computer games.
3 They ...... to the cinema.
4 She ...... to music.
5 She ...... the Internet.
6 They ...... volleyball.

1 Label the pictures with the words in the box.

> cheerful   confident   lazy   loud   nasty
> serious   ~~shy~~

shy

1

2

3

4

5

6

GRAMMAR

→ Student's Book pages 6 and 8

Present tense contrast

1 Complete the sentences. Use the present simple or present continuous.

1 Look at Liam. He _____ (dance).

2 Put your coat on. It _____ (not snow), but it's cold.

3 They _____ (not play) computer games during the week.

4 She _____ (do) karate on Saturday afternoons.

5 Look, I _____ (wear) a new top.

6 He _____ (not like) sport.

2 Complete the email with the verbs in the box. Use the present simple or present continuous.

Hi James

How are you? I hope you (**1** enjoy) _____ _____ the winter in the UK. There's lots of snow here in Colorado. In fact, it (**2** snow) _____ at the moment! We (**3** go) _____ skiing every Saturday morning. It's great!

My sister Jodie has got a new hobby – dancing. She (**4** have) _____ lessons every weekend and she (**5** practise) _____ every evening in her room. It's really noisy tonight and I (**6** try) _____ to work in here!

I (**7** send) _____ you a photo of me and my sister in the mountains. I (**8** wear) _____ my new skiing clothes. They're cool, aren't they?

Chuck

Revision: past simple affirmative

3 Complete the text with the past simple affirmative. Be careful – some verbs are regular and some are irregular.

I **went** (go) to a really exciting football match last weekend. It was Manchester United and Real Madrid. We (**1**) _____ (arrive) at the stadium at 7.30. We (**2**) _____ (buy) some chips and some Coke. Then we (**3**) _____ (find) our seats. The match (**4**) _____ (start) at 7.45.

My dad is a Manchester United fan. When Real Madrid (**5**) _____ (score), my dad (**6**) _____ (drop) his chips. He was really annoyed. But in the end, Manchester United (**7**) _____ (win) 4–3. Both teams (**8**) _____ (play) really well – and my dad was pleased with the result!

4 Complete the sentences about Tim's year using the past simple affirmative of the verbs in the box.

break   chat   ~~find~~   leave   meet   play
remember   watch   win

He **found** £40 in his coat pocket.

1 Only one friend _____ his birthday.

2 His sister _____ his computer, and now he can't use it.

3 He _____ to the most attractive girl in town.

4 His favourite teacher _____ the school.

5 He _____ a great film with his friends.

6 He _____ a really interesting girl at a party.

7 His favourite football team _____ the league.

8 He _____ volleyball on the beach.

Revision: comparative and superlative adjectives

5 Complete the sentences with the comparative. Decide if you agree or disagree.

Will Young is popular, but Robbie Williams is **more popular**.
☑ I agree ☐ I disagree

1 Christina Aguilera is beautiful, but Jennifer Lopez is _____ .
☐ I agree ☐ I disagree

2 Jim Carrey is funny, but Mike Myers is _____ .
☐ I agree ☐ I disagree

3 Manchester United are successful, but Real Madrid are _____ .
☐ I agree ☐ I disagree

4 Chocolate is nice, but fruit is _____ .
☐ I agree ☐ I disagree

5 History is interesting, but geography is _____ .
☐ I agree ☐ I disagree

6 Johnny Depp is a good actor, but Brad Pitt is _____ .
☐ I agree ☐ I disagree

6 Write sentences. Use the comparative form of the adjectives and *than*.

Liam / tall / Helen
Liam is taller than Helen.

1 I / lazy / my brother
_____

2 Tom / confident / Karen
_____

3 Simon / impatient / his sister
_____

4 August / hot / May
_____

5 my mum / funny / my dad
_____

6 London / big / Manchester
_____

7 Complete the sentences. Use the superlative form of the adjectives in the box.

big   expensive   far   high   lazy

1 Pluto is the _____ planet from the sun.

2 Diamonds are the _____ stones in the world.

3 Koala bears are the _____ animals in the world.

4 Mount Everest is the _____ mountain in the world.

5 Jupiter is the _____ planet in the solar system.

Revision: *should / shouldn't*

8 Give advice to these people. Write sentences with *should* or *shouldn't* and the phrases in the box.

eat it   have something to eat
open a window   put on a jacket
stay up late   tell anyone

1 I'm really tired.
_____

2 I'm hot.
_____

3 I'm hungry.
_____

4 This pizza is terrible!
_____

5 I'm cold.
_____

6 It's a secret!
_____

EVERYDAY ENGLISH

Dialogue

→ Student's Book page 7

1 Complete the conversation with the sentences in the box.

> Are you doing anything on Friday evening?
> Do you want to come?
> How are you?   What time are you meeting?
> Why don't we ask Lucy, too?

TALKING ABOUT ARRANGEMENTS

Jake Hi, Susan. This is Jake.
(1) _____

Susan I'm well, thanks. And you?

Jake I'm fine. (2) _____

Susan I don't think so. Why?

Jake I'm going bowling with my cousins.
(3) _____

Susan I'd love to. Thanks!

Jake Great! (4) _____

Susan Yes, that's a good idea.

Jake We're getting a bus from the High Street.

Susan (5) _____

Jake Eight o'clock.

Susan Great! See you there!

2 Complete the summary of Jake and Susan's arrangement.

They're going (1) _____ with Jake's
(2) _____ . They're also inviting
(3) _____ . They're meeting at
(4) _____ o'clock on (5) _____
evening. They're travelling by (6) _____ .

3 In your notebook, write a conversation like the one in exercise 1.

A _____

_____

B _____

_____

A _____

B _____

A _____

_____

B _____

A _____

_____

B _____

A _____

_____

B _____

A _____

B _____

1 Incredible journeys

VOCABULARY

Transport

→ Student's Book page 9

1 Complete the puzzle.

1→ 1↓ 2→

3↓ 4→ 5→

6→ 7↓ 8→

```
  ¹→
  ↓B □ □ □

  ²→ ³
   S ↓H □ □

  ⁴→
   P □ □ □ □

      ⁵→
       C □ □ □

  ⁶→
   M □ □ □ □

          ⁷
          ↓B
  ⁸→
   T □ □ □ □
          □
          □
```

2 Write true answers.

1 How do you get to school?
_____

2 How long does it take?
_____

3 Who do you go with?
_____

4 How do you get to town at weekends?
_____

5 How long does it take?
_____

6 Who do you go wlth?
_____

Word check Travel words

→ Student's Book page 11

3 Complete the instructions with the travel words in the box.

> arrives   bus stop   catch   leaves
> stops   ticket

Getting to the stadium

The first train to Liverpool (**1**) _____ London at 8.00 in the morning. You can buy your (**2**) _____ on the train. The train (**3**) _____ at Oxford and Birmingham. Don't get off! It (**4**) _____ in Liverpool at 13.25. When you arrive, (**5**) _____ a number 26 bus to Anfield Football Station. The (**6**) _____ is opposite the train station.

GRAMMAR

Past simple negative and interrogative

→ Student's Book pages 12 and 14

1 Put the words in the correct order to make negative sentences.

1 to / didn't / yesterday / they / school / go

_____

2 didn't / she / lunch / finish / her

_____

3 train / stop / the / didn't

_____

4 come / to / they / my / didn't / party

_____

5 hotel / I / stay / didn't / a / in

_____

6 travel / helicopter / by / didn't / you

_____

7 TV / I / weekend / watch / last / didn't

_____

2 Look at the pictures and correct the sentences. Use one negative and one affirmative form.

He played football yesterday. (go swimming)
He didn't play football. He went swimming.

1 She caught a train to school on Monday. (walk)

_____

_____

2 They won the football match. (lose)

_____

_____

3 The boat arrived in Sydney. (sink)

_____

_____

4 She did her homework last night. (watch TV)

_____

_____

5 They left early. (stay until one o'clock)

_____

_____

6 He went to the cinema at eight o'clock.
(have dinner with his family)

_____

_____

3 Write five things you *didn't* do last weekend.

1 _____

2 _____

3 _____

4 _____

5 _____

4 Look at the chart. Write questions and answers about what they did last Saturday.

	morning	afternoon
Sally	💿	🚌
Andy	⚽	🚲
Laura and Mark	👥	🥋

Sally / listen to music?
Did Sally listen to music? Yes, she did.

1 Andy / catch a bus?

_____

_____

2 Laura and Mark / do karate?

_____

_____

3 Sally / meet her friends?

_____

_____

4 Andy / play football?

_____

_____

5 Laura and Mark / go cycling?

_____

_____

5 Complete the questions. Then write your own answers for the questions.

1 What time _____ (you / get up) this morning?

_____

2 What _____ (you / have) for breakfast?

_____

3 Who _____ (you / sit) next to in your last English lesson?

_____

4 Where _____ (you / go) to school last year?

_____

Prepositions of movement

6 Put the sentences in the correct order. Then tick (✔) the correct picture.

1 up / ran / she / mountain / a

_____

2 bridge / he / across / walked / a

_____

3 wall / down / climbed / a / she

_____

4 bed / a / ran / they / under

_____

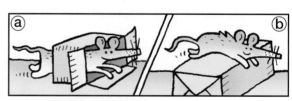

5 box / it / a / ran / through

_____

6 walked / street / she / across / a

_____

EVERYDAY ENGLISH

Dialogue

→ Student's Book page 13

1 Complete the conversation. Use the sentences in the box.

> Which platform is it?   You're welcome.
> Single or return?   Thanks.

AT THE TRAIN STATION

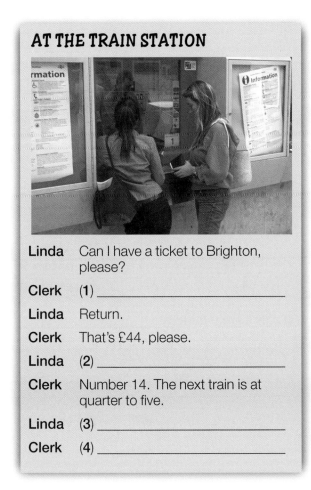

Linda Can I have a ticket to Brighton, please?

Clerk (1) _____

Linda Return.

Clerk That's £44, please.

Linda (2) _____

Clerk Number 14. The next train is at quarter to five.

Linda (3) _____

Clerk (4) _____

2 Write another conversation like the one in exercise 1.

Juan _____

_____

Clerk _____

Juan _____

Clerk _____

Juan _____

Clerk _____

_____

Juan _____

Clerk _____

READING AND WRITING

Reading

3 Read the text. Label the cities on the map.

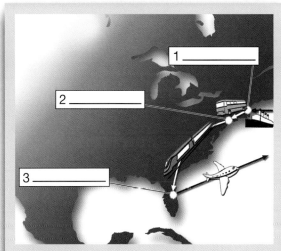

Holiday in the USA

Last summer, James Wilson won an amazing holiday to the USA in a competition. First, he travelled from London to Boston by boat. He saw dolphins in the sea near Boston. Then he caught a bus to New York. He went up the Empire State Building and took lots of photos.

After that, he went to Orlando by train. He visited Universal Studios and Sea World. In James' opinion, it was the most exciting part of the holiday. Finally, after two weeks in the USA, James went home to London by plane.

4 Read the text again. Answer the questions.

1 Why did James go to the USA?

_____

2 Where did he see dolphins?

_____

3 How did he travel to New York?

_____

4 What two places did he visit in Orlando?

_____

5 How long was he in the USA?

_____

Writing Ordering events

→ Student's Book page 15

5 Complete the paragraph with the words in the box.

> after that   finally   first   then

> Last Saturday, I went to London with my aunt. **(1)** _____ , we caught the train to Victoria Station. It took about two hours. **(2)** _____ we went to Covent Garden by underground. We did a lot of shopping! **(3)** _____ we had lunch in a restaurant. **(4)** _____ we caught the train home again.

6 Look at the map and the information. Write a description of the journey.

> London – visit Madame Tussaud
> go shopping in Oxford Street
> Liverpool – watch a football match
> Cardiff – see the castle

Holiday in the UK

Last month, Ana González won a fantastic holiday to the UK. First, she _____ from Buenos Aires to _____ . She visited _____ and she _____ _____ . Then, she _____ . She _____ _____ .

It was really exciting!

After that, Ana _____ _____ .

The journey took four hours. In Cardiff, she _____ .

Finally, she _____ _____ .

It was a great holiday.

LEARNING DIARY

1 Complete the chart.

		Yes	No
Vocabulary	I can name six means of transport.		
	I can describe a journey by train or bus, using travel words like *bus stop*, *ticket*, *catch*, *arrive*.		
Grammar	I can make past simple negative sentences.		
	I can ask questions about the past.		
	I can name four prepositions of movement and know how to use them.		
Speaking	I know how to book a train ticket.		
Writing	I can write five sentences about an incredible journey.		

2 Mystery

VOCABULARY

In the home

→ Student's Book ▸ page 17

1 Complete the puzzle.

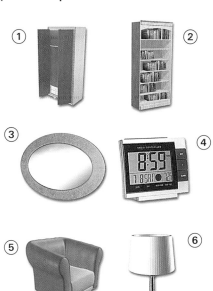

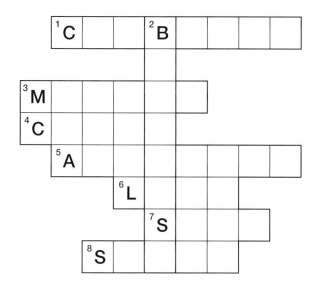

```
¹C _ _ _ ²B _ _ _ _ _
        ³M _ _ _
        ⁴C _ _
          ⁵A _ _ _ _ _ _
            ⁶L _ _ _
              ⁷S _ _ _ _
            ⁸S _ _ _ _
```

Word check Parts of a house

→ Student's Book ▸ page 19

2 In which parts of the house can you find these things?

1 in the living room   2 _____

3 _____   4 _____

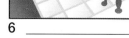

5 _____   6 _____

7 _____   8 _____

GRAMMAR

Past continuous

→ Student's Book ▶ pages 20 and 22 ▶

1 Complete the sentences. Use the past continuous affirmative.

1 Jack _____ (wear) a blue jacket.

2 We didn't play tennis because it _____ (rain).

3 They _____ (sit) in the living room.

4 I _____ (play) the guitar at six o'clock last night.

5 She _____ (dance) in the kitchen!

6 You _____ (laugh). Was it funny?

7 The sun _____ (shine) yesterday so we went to the beach.

2 Write negative sentences. Use the past continuous.

she / not worry / about the exams
She wasn't worrying about the exams.

1 They / not surf / the Internet

_____

2 The train / not go / to London

_____

3 You / not listen / to the teacher

_____

4 We / not live / in England in 1999

_____

5 She / not get / dressed for the party

_____

6 I / not argue / with my mum

_____

7 My dad / not cook / dinner / in the kitchen

_____

_____

3 Look at the photo and correct the sentences. Write one negative sentence and one affirmative sentence.

Carol   Lucy

Carol was drinking cola.
Carol wasn't drinking cola. She was drinking water.

1 Lucy and Carol were sitting on armchairs.

_____

_____

2 Lucy was watching TV.

_____

_____

3 Lucy was wearing a shirt.

_____

_____

4 Carol was reading a newspaper.

_____

_____

5 Lucy was eating crisps.

_____

_____

6 Lucy and Carol were wearing tracksuit bottoms.

_____

_____

Lord Melbury was on the floor in the library. He was dead …

Mrs Brown

Lady Parker

Sir George Parker

Albert   Edward

Lady Melbury

Sophie   Annabel

4 Look at the pictures. Write questions and short answers.

1 Sir George Parker / read / in the kitchen?

_____

_____

2 Lady Melbury / write / a letter?

_____

_____

3 Lady Parker / play the cello?

_____

_____

4 Albert and Edward / sit / in the garden?

_____

_____

5 Mrs Brown / prepare / dinner?

_____

_____

6 Sophie and Annabel / have / tea?

_____

_____

5 Answer the questions.

1 What were you doing at ten o'clock yesterday morning?

_____

_____

_____

2 What were you doing at eight o'clock last night?

_____

_____

_____

3 What were your parents doing at three o'clock yesterday afternoon?

_____

_____

_____

4 What was your friend doing at half past six yesterday evening?

_____

_____

EVERYDAY ENGLISH

Dialogue

→ Student's Book page 21

1 Put the lines in the correct order.

ASKING FOR AND GIVING PERMISSION

- ☐ **Kate** Great! Can we go to the party after that?
- ☐ **Kate** Oh, OK.
- ☐ **Kate** Can I go to the café with Luisa this evening?
- ☐ **Kate** Why not?
- ☐ **Mum** No, you can't. Sorry.
- ☐ **Mum** Because it's Monday tomorrow and you've got a lot of homework.
- ☐ **Mum** Yes, sure. That's a nice idea.

2 Write a conversation like the one in exercise 1.

Miguel _____

_____

Dad _____

Miguel _____

_____

Dad _____

Miguel _____

Dad _____

_____

Miguel _____

READING AND WRITING

Reading

3 Read the text.

A strange meeting

Last summer I went to Raglan Castle with my family. It was a lovely day. It was hot and the sun was shining. I walked along the wall at the top of the castle with my brother, John. Suddenly, we saw a woman. She was standing in front of us. Her clothes were very old and strange. She was wearing a long white dress and a tall hat. She said to me, 'What have you got in your hand?'

'It's a camera,' I said, and I showed it to her.

'Can we take a photo of you?' asked my brother.

'Yes, if you want to,' said the woman. When I looked at the screen on my camera, the woman wasn't there!

Kate

4 Answer the questions.

1 Where did Kate go last summer?

_____

2 What was the weather like?

_____

3 Who did they see?

_____

4 Where was the woman standing?

_____

5 What was she wearing?

_____

6 What did John want to do?

_____

7 Why was it a strange experience?

_____

Writing *so*

→ Student's Book ▷ page 23

5 Match the sentences, and join them with *so*.

1	I was tired.	**a)** I went to London.
2	The joke wasn't funny.	**b)** I went to bed.
3	He was cold.	**c)** They were scared.
4	They saw a ghost.	**d)** He put on his jacket.
5	I wanted to visit Madame Tussauds.	**e)** We didn't laugh.

1 – b **I was tired, so I went to bed.**

2 _____

3 _____

4 _____

5 _____

6 Write a story. Use the text in exercise 3 and the ideas in the box to help you.

> a camcorder   Dudley Castle   cold
> a long blue jacket and a big black hat
> a man   raining   my sister   take a film
> walk in the garden

Last winter I _____ with _____ . It was _____ day and it was _____ . I _____ with _____ . Suddenly, _____ . He was _____ of us. His clothes were _____ . He was wearing _____ . He said to me, '_____ hand?'

'It's _____', I said, and I _____ .

'Can _____?' asked _____ .

'_____' said the man. When _____ , the man _____ !

LEARNING DIARY

1 Complete the chart.

		Yes	No
Vocabulary	I can name four things you find in the home.		
	I can name six parts of a house.		
Grammar	I know the affirmative, negative and interrogative forms of the past continuous.		
Pronunciation	I can pronounce the weak forms /wəz/ and /wə(r)/ correctly.		
Speaking	I know how to ask for and give permission.		
Writing	I can write four sentences about an imaginary strange experience.		

3 Our world

VOCABULARY

The natural world

→ Student's Book page 29

1 Look at the photos and complete the sentences. Use two words from the box for each sentence.

> beach island lake mountains river sea valley

1 There's an _____ in the middle of the _____ .

2 There's _____ near the _____ .

3 There's a _____ in the _____ .

4 There are birds on the _____ .

2 Match these natural features with words in the box from exercise 1.

Copacabana **beach**

1 Amazon _____
2 Titicaca _____
3 The Andes _____
4 Mediterranean _____
5 The Galapagos _____

Word check Wildlife

→ Student's Book page 31

3 Label the pictures.

> bear camel eagle fly
> lion shark tiger whale

1 _____

2 _____

3 _____

4 _____

5 _____

6 _____

7 _____

8 _____

GRAMMAR

Countable and uncountable nouns

→ Student's Book pages 32 and 34

1 Are the words 'countable' or 'uncountable'?

	Countable	Uncountable
food		✔
1 mountain		
2 lake		
3 cheese		
4 orange juice		
5 sandwich		
6 homework		
7 bread		
8 apple		
9 rice		
10 beach		

2 Choose the correct sentence.

1 **a)** I like biscuit.

b) I like biscuits.

2 **a)** She doesn't eat a pasta.

b) She doesn't eat pasta.

3 **a)** We usually drink milk at breakfast.

b) We usually drink milks at breakfast.

4 **a)** Do you want sandwich?

b) Do you want a sandwich?

5 **a)** Money isn't the most important thing in life.

b) A money isn't the most important thing in life.

6 **a)** Can I have a litre of waters, please?

b) Can I have a litre of water, please?

some and *any*

3 Look at Rachel and Johnny's shopping. Write affirmative or negative sentences with *bought* or *didn't buy*, and *some* or *any*.

Rachel / cheese
Rachel didn't buy any cheese.

Johnny / cheese
Johnny bought some cheese.

1 Rachel / bread

_____

2 Johnny / milk

_____

3 Rachel / grapes

_____

4 Johnny / bananas

_____

5 Rachel / cereal

_____

6 Johnny / magazines

_____

4 Write affirmative, negative or interrogative sentences in the past simple. Remember to include *some* or *any*.

you / see / good films / last week?
Did you see any good films last week?

1 we / not have / homework / yesterday

_____

2 my mum / make / bread / at the weekend

_____

3 I / phone / friends / last night

_____

4 you / buy / books / in town?

_____

How much / How many …?

5 Complete the questions with *How much* or
How many. Then answer the questions.

How many pets has Jack got?
Five.

1 _____ questions did Sarah get wrong?

_____ .

2 _____ orange juice has he got?

_____ .

3 _____ pizzas did they eat?

_____ .

4 _____ homework is she giving her
students?

_____ .

5 _____ legs has a spider got?

_____ .

should / shouldn't

6 Match the sentences with the pictures. Then
complete them with *should* or *shouldn't*.

1 They _____ take an umbrella. Picture ___
2 They _____ swim in the sea. Picture ___
3 She _____ buy a new bike. Picture ___
4 It _____ be on the table. Picture ___
5 He _____ sing in public. Picture ___
6 He _____ go to school. Picture ___

7 Write true sentences.

My best friend should …

_____

_____ .

My best friend shouldn't …

_____

_____

Dialogue

→ Student's Book page 33

1 Complete the conversation with the words in the box.

> go to school   How are you?
> I've got a headache.   What's the matter?
> You're right.

GIVING ADVICE

Mary Hi, Sam. **(1)** _____

Sam Not great.

Mary Oh. **(2)** _____

Sam I'm really hot and **(3)** _____

Mary I don't think you should **(4)** _____
      today. I think you should phone the doctor.

Sam **(5)** _____

2 Write another conversation like the one in exercise 1. Use the summary in the box to help you.

> David's problem – he feels sick and he's got a stomach ache.
> Florencia's advice – don't go the party, stay at home.

Florencia _____

David   _____

Florencia _____

David   _____

     _____

Florencia _____

     _____

     _____

David   _____

Reading

3 Look at the photo and read the text.

Patagonia is a great place for a holiday. It's in the south of Argentina. Two big towns there are Trelew and Comodoro Rivadavia. There are lots of smaller towns and villages too. The beaches are beautiful and very popular with tourists. There are also mountains and rivers. People come to go skiing nearby in Bariloche in Winter.

Some of the best beaches in the region are in the Valdez Peninsula. A lot of people visit the Valdez Peninsula because it's a fantastic place for scuba-diving. The water is cold but there are lots of interesting things to see. There are whales and sea lions here.

4 Answer the questions.

1 Where is Patagonia?

   _____

2 What are the main towns?

   _____

3 Are there any mountains?

   _____

4 Why do a lot of people visit the Valdez Peninsula?

   _____

5 What can you see there?

   _____

Writing Preparing to write

→ **Student's Book** page 35

5 Complete the notes about a nature park.

> beautiful mountains and rivers   forests
> Tierra del Fuego   no, but a campsite
> albatross and other interesting birds
> red foxes   walking, animal-watching

name of nature park:	
big hotels:	
natural features:	
activities:	
wildlife:	

6 Complete the text. Use the notes from Exercise 5. Include *some* or *any*.

Another great place is _____

_____ . It's a nature park in the most

southern part of South America. There _____

_____ hotels, but _____ .

There _____

and rivers in the park, and there are also

_____ . You can go _____

_____ there. There's interesting wildlife

too. You _____ albatross and

_____ .

LEARNING DIARY

1 Complete the chart.

		Yes	No
Vocabulary	I can name five parts of 'the natural world'.		
	I can name five wild animals.		
Grammar	I know the difference between countable and uncountable nouns.		
	I can use *some* and *any* correctly.		
	I know when to use *How much?* and when to use *How many?*		
Pronunciation	I know the correct intonation for yes/no questions and statements.		
Speaking	I know how to give advice.		
Writing	I can write four sentences about a region of my country.		

4 Going out

VOCABULARY

Places to go

→ Student's Book page 37

1 Complete the labels.

1 p _ _ _ _

2 m _ _ _ _ _

3 a _ _ _ _ _ _ _ _ a _ _ _ _ _

4 t _ _ _ _ p _ _ _

5 r _ _ _ _ _ _ _ _

6 I _ _ _ _ _ _ _ c _ _ _

7 s _ _ _ _ _ _ p _ _ _

8 a _ _ _ _ _ _ _

2 Answer the questions.

1 Where can you play computer games?

At an _____

2 Where can you see fish?

_____

3 Where can you dance and chat with your friends?

_____

4 Where can you surf the Internet?

_____

5 Where can you see famous paintings?

_____

6 Where can you have lunch?

_____

7 Where can you go swimming?

_____

8 Where can you go on rides?

_____

Word check Food and drink

→ Student's Book page 39

3 Find seven foods and five drinks in the word square.

F	O	W	L	P	A	B	U	R	G	E	R
S	M	A	U	I	Y	D	T	C	H	O	L
H	O	T	C	H	O	C	O	L	A	T	E
C	H	E	E	S	E	R	V	I	K	B	M
H	C	R	I	S	P	S	A	F	Y	R	O
I	B	U	L	T	C	H	I	C	K	E	N
P	O	S	A	N	D	W	I	C	H	A	A
S	P	C	O	L	A	U	R	I	G	D	D
T	R	A	P	P	L	E	J	U	I	C	E

GRAMMAR

going to and future time expressions

→ **Student's Book** ▸ **pages 40 and 42** ▸

1 Write sentences with *going to* affirmative.

1 She / have lunch / in town

_____

2 We / go swimming / next Saturday

_____

_____

3 I / surf the Internet / this evening

_____

4 They / visit the aquarium / tomorrow
afternoon

_____

_____

5 You / meet me / at the museum

_____

6 It / rain / tomorrow

_____

2 Complete the future time expressions. Use *next* or *tomorrow*.

1 _____ week

2 _____ afternoon

3 _____ year

4 _____ morning

5 _____ evening

6 _____ month

7 _____ Saturday

3 Answer the questions. Write true answers.

1 What are you going to do on Saturday
evening?

_____

_____

_____

2 What are you going to do in the summer
holidays?

_____

_____

_____

4 Make the sentences in exercise 1 negative.

1 **She isn't going to have** _____

_____

2 _____

_____

3 _____

4 _____

_____

5 _____

6 _____

5 Complete the sentences. Use *going to*
negative and the verbs in the box.

| buy | fly | go out | have | meet | walk |

1 I _____ this evening
because I've got a lot of homework.

2 She's ill so she _____
her friends at the theme park.

3 They _____ to school.
They're going to go by bike.

4 We haven't got much money so we
_____ a new DVD player.

5 I hate planes so I _____
to England.

6 He isn't hungry so he
_____ _____ lunch.

6 Complete the conversations. Write questions with *going to*.

Boy What / you / do on Friday evening?

What are you going to do on Friday evening?

Girl I'm going to go to the cinema.

Boy What film / you / see?

(1) _____

_____

Girl The new Viggo Mortensen film.

Boy Who / you / go with?

(2) _____

_____

Girl Mark and Jane.

Boy How / you / get there?

(3) _____

_____

Girl We're going to go by bus.

Boy What / you / do after the film?

(4) _____

_____

Girl We're going to go for a pizza.

Boy What time / you / arrive home?

(5) _____

_____

Girl At about eleven o'clock.

must / mustn't

7 Compete the sentences with *must* or *mustn't*.

1 We _____ do our homework on time.

2 You _____ shout in class.

3 It's late. I _____ go home.

4 He's got a lot of homework. He _____ go out this evening.

5 We _____ swim here. It's dangerous.

6 It's a secret. You _____ tell anybody.

8 Jane is going to have a party. Look at the instructions that her parents gave her. Write sentences with *must* and *mustn't*.

1 **You mustn't dance on the sofa.**

2 _____

_____

3 _____

_____

4 _____

_____

5 _____

_____

6 _____

_____

Jane

1 Don't dance on the sofa.

2 Don't take drinks into the living room.

3 Wash up after the party.

4 Tidy the house before we come back.

5 Go to bed before midnight.

6 Don't be noisy!

Have a great party.

Love

Mum and Dad

EVERYDAY ENGLISH

READING AND WRITING

Dialogue

→ Student's Book page 41

1 Complete the conversation with the sentences in the box.

> And for you?   Anything to drink?
> Can I have an orange juice, please?
> Can I help you?   Here you are.

IN A CAFÉ

Menu

Food	Drinks
Cheese and tomato sandwich £2.50	Apple juice £1.50
Egg sandwich .. £2.25	Orange juice £1.50
Baked potato & cheese £3.00	Milkshake £1.25

Waiter	Hi. **(1)** _____
Boy	Can I have an egg sandwich, please?
Waiter	Sure. **(2)** _____
Girl	A cheese and tomato sandwich for me, please.
Waiter	**(3)** _____
Boy	A milkshake for me, please.
Girl	**(4)** _____
Waiter	That's £7.50, please.
Boy	**(5)** _____
Waiter	Thank you.

2 Write another conversation like the one in exercise 1. Use the food and drink in the menu.

Waiter _____

Boy _____

Waiter _____

Girl _____

Waiter _____

Boy _____

Girl _____

Waiter _____

Boy _____

Waiter _____

Reading

3 Read the text.

Plans for the weekend

I'm going to have a really busy weekend.

On Saturday morning, I'm going to meet my friends in town. We're going to go shopping. I can't find my black top so I must buy a new one.

On Saturday afternoon, I'm going to see the new Johnny Depp film with my brother. After that we're going to go to the Internet café.

I'm going to stay in on Saturday evening. There's a concert on TV with Justin Timberlake.

On Sunday, we're going to visit my grandparents. They live in a small village near the sea. We're all going to have lunch in a restaurant. My grandad has got a great computer so in the afternoon my brother and I are going to play games on it.

Finally, on Sunday evening, I'm going to do my homework. Boring!

What are you going to do this weekend?

Carmen

4 Put the events in the correct order.

a) ☐ visit her grandparents

b) ☐ do her homework

c) ☐ buy a new top

d) ☐ watch a concert on TV

e) ☐ surf the Internet

f) ☐ play computer games

g) ☐ go to the cinema

h) ☐ have lunch in a restaurant

Writing Using pronouns

→ Student's Book page 43

5 Complete the sentences. Use the pronouns in the box.

he	her	him	she	them	we

1 Pete is going to the amusement arcade. Are you going to go with _____ .

2 I love Shakira. _____ is my favourite singer.

3 My grandparents live in New Zealand. I'm going to visit _____ next Christmas.

4 Luis and I are going to the disco this evening. _____ are going to meet there at eight o'clock.

5 That's Sonia's pen. Give it to _____ .

6 It's Jack's birthday on Saturday. _____ is going to be 14.

6 Write about your plans for the weekend.

On Saturday morning, _____
_____
_____ .
_____

On Saturday afternoon, _____
_____
_____
_____ .

On Sunday, _____
_____
_____
_____
_____ .

LEARNING DIARY

1 Complete the chart.

		Yes	No
Vocabulary	I can name four places to go.		
	I can name four drinks and four items of food.		
Grammar	I can talk about future plans using *going to*.		
	I know how to use *must* and *mustn't* correctly.		
Pronunciation	I can pronounce contractions like *couldn't* and *mustn't* correctly.		
Speaking	I know how to order food and drink in a cafe.		
Writing	I can write an invitation to a birthday party.		

5 The future

VOCABULARY

Computers

→ Student's Book ⟩ page 45 ⟩

1 Do the puzzle.

Across (→)

1 We use these to listen to music and sounds.

3 We use this to provide video pictures for a computer.

4 We use this to move around the screen.

5 We use this to scan pictures into a computer.

6 We use this to print out copies of our work.

7 We can store information on this.

Down (↓)

1 This is the part we look at.

2 We use this to type information into a computer.

Word check Computer studies

→ Student's Book ⟩ page 47 ⟩

2 Complete the phrases with the nouns in the box.

| CD   disk   picture   software |
| text   website |

1 install _____

2 burn a _____

3 visit a _____

4 type a _____

5 eject a _____

6 scan a _____

GRAMMAR

will

→ Student's Book   pages 48 and 50

1 Look at the list. Write sentences about Cathy's future.

	go to university	✗
1	be rich	✔
2	travel around the world	✔
3	work in a city	✗
4	meet famous people	✗
5	have a Ferrari	✔

She won't go to university.

1 _____
2 _____
3 _____
4 _____
5 _____

2 Complete the chart and make predictions about your future. Write sentences with *will* or *won't*.

Will you ...	Yes	No
1 live in another country?		
2 get married?		
3 have children?		
4 be a pop star?		
5 have a pet?		

1 _____
2 _____
3 _____
4 _____
5 _____

3 Complete the questions and answers.

Will it rain (it / rain) tomorrow?
Yes, **it will**.

1 _____ (she / be) a doctor?
No, _____ .

2 _____ (he / pass) the exam?
Yes, _____ .

3 _____ (they / come) to the party?
No, _____ .

4 _____ (your brother / like) his present?
Yes, _____ .

5 _____ (your parents / stay) at home?
No, _____ .

6 _____ (it / be) sunny tomorrow?
No, _____ .

4 Complete the questions about your future. Then give your own answers.

1 _____ (where / you / live) when you're 25?

_____

2 _____ (who / you / live with)?

_____

3 _____ (where / you / work)?

_____

4 _____ (what / you / do)?

_____

5 _____ (how many children / you / have)?

_____

6 _____ (what / car / you / have)?

_____

First conditional

5 Look at the pictures. Complete the sentences with *will* and the phrases in the box.

> be angry   break it   catch the bus   feel ill
> remember his holiday   win the game

If he jumps in the water, the sharks **will eat him**.

1 If she arrives late, her teacher _____
_____ .

2 If he takes some photos, he _____
_____ .

3 If they play well, they _____
_____ .

4 If she drops the computer, she _____
_____ .

5 If he eats all three pizzas, he _____
_____ .

6 If she runs, she _____
_____ .

6 Complete the sentences using the present simple, affirmative or negative, of the verbs.

1 If they _____ (go) to school, they won't learn anything.

2 If he _____ (install) some new software, his computer will work better.

3 If this scanner (work) _____ , I'll buy a new one.

4 If it _____ (rain) tomorrow, we'll have a picnic.

5 If she _____ (catch) a bus, she'll get home before dinner.

6 If they _____ (find) a restaurant, they won't have lunch.

EVERYDAY ENGLISH

Dialogue

→ Student's Book page 49

1 Complete the conversation. Use the sentences in the box.

> Do you want anything to eat?   I'll wait here.
> Here's your change.   Here you are.

AT THE CINEMA

Man Can I help you?
Lisa Yes. I'd like two tickets for *Running Game*.
Man That's £6.40, please.
Lisa (1) _____
Man Thank you. (2) _____
The film starts in five minutes. It's screen five.
Lisa OK. Thanks.
Peter I'm going to buy some crisps.
(3) _____
Lisa No, but I'll have something to drink.
Peter OK. I'll buy a bottle of lemonade.
Lisa Thanks. (4) _____

2 Write another conversation like the one in exercise 1. Use the ideas in the box.

> a sandwich   film – Lost in Space
> orange juice   tickets – £4.10 each
> starts screen two in 10 minutes

Man _____
Ana _____
_____
Man _____
Ana _____
Man _____
_____
Ana _____
Man _____
_____
Ana _____
Man _____
Ana _____

READING AND WRITING

Reading

3 Read the text. Label the two paragraphs with two of these headings.

Free time   Home   Work   Education

City of the future

(1) _____

Children will go to school, but there won't be any teachers. Students will use computers, and robots will answer all of their questions. Students won't have homework because they'll work hard in the classroom. They'll pass all of their exams.

(2) _____

Adults will have jobs, but they won't work very hard. Robots will do all the dangerous or boring jobs. The most important people will be computer programmers. They'll earn a lot of money. A lot of people will work at home, but some people will work in offices.

4 Answer the questions.

1 Will children go to school?
_____

2 Why won't students have homework?
_____

3 Will students pass all their exams?
_____

4 Who will be the most important people?
_____

5 Will everybody work at home?
_____

Writing Using paragraphs

→ Student's Book page 51

5 Match these notes with the other two paragraph headings from exercise 3.

1 people / eat / in cafés – waiters / be / robots   **Free time**

2 apartments / be / very modern – robots / clean / the rooms   _____

3 children / play football / in parks – adults / go cycling / in the mountains – everybody / be / very healthy   _____

4 people / not go / to the cinema – they / take part / in reality TV programmes   _____

5 fridge / have / computers – food / arrive / automatically   _____

6 homes / have / phones and TVs / in every room   _____

6 Write the other two paragraphs of the text. Use the notes from exercise 5.

City of the future

_____

_____

_____

_____

_____

_____

_____

_____

_____

_____

_____

_____

LEARNING DIARY

1 Complete the chart.

		Yes	No
Vocabulary	I can name five parts of a computer.		
	I know the meaning of the verbs *scan*, *install* and *burn* and can use them with the correct nouns.		
Grammar	I can make predictions about the future using *will* and *won't*.		
	I know how to form first conditional sentences.		
Pronunciation	I know how to say simple sentences with the correct rhythm and stress.		
Speaking	I know how to book cinema tickets.		
Writing	I can write four sentences about a space colony.		

OXFORD
UNIVERSITY PRESS

Great Clarendon Street, Oxford OX2 6DP

Oxford University Press is a department of the University of Oxford.
It furthers the University's objective of excellence in research, scholarship,
and education by publishing worldwide in

Oxford New York

Auckland Cape Town Dar es Salaam Hong Kong Karachi
Kuala Lumpur Madrid Melbourne Mexico City Nairobi
New Delhi Shanghai Taipei Toronto

With offices in

Argentina Austria Brazil Chile Czech Republic France Greece
Guatemala Hungary Italy Japan Poland Portugal Singapore
South Korea Switzerland Thailand Turkey Ukraine Vietnam

OXFORD and OXFORD ENGLISH are registered trade marks of
Oxford University Press in the UK and in certain other countries

ISBN: 978 0 19 415318 8

Printed in China

ACKNOWLEDGEMENTS

The authors would like to thank everyone who has helped in the creation
and production of this book, especially the staff of Oxford University Press in
Oxford and Spain. We are also very grateful to our project manager,
Desmond O'Sullivan of ELT Publishing Services. Our thanks also go to: Chris
King for photographing the photostory and Helen Reilly of Arnos Design for
managing the illustrations and the researched photography.

Project management by: Desmond O'Sullivan, ELT Publishing Services.

*The publishers and authors would like to thank all the teachers who have contributed to
the development of this course, in particular*: Maria Cristina Koffler, Colegio Juan
Segundo Fernandez; Genoveva Barsanti, Colegio Nuestra Señora del Rosario;
Mariela Elinger, Colegio Nuestra Señora de la Misericordia; Leticia Viarenghi,
Colegio Nuestra Raíces; Adriana Perez, Instituto French; Lilian Berrogain,
Colegio Ramos Mejía; Maria Marta Mora, Instituto Velez Sarfield; Patricia
Mandel, Instituto Smile; Silvia Flores, Colegio Leon XIII.

Illustrations by:
Adrian Barclay pp. 88 (ex 5), 91; Michael Butler/Thoughtscape pp, 27 (ex 8),
42, 52; Cybèle/Three in a Box p. 5; Emma Dodd pp. 76; Bruno Drummond
pp. 20, 25 (ex 3), 34 (ex 2), 40, 45, 50; Mark Duffin pp. 34, 81 (ex 1), 84, 96;
Richard Duszczak pp. 5, 8, 72 (ex 2); Spike Gerrell pp. 72 (ex 1), 77, 78, 83,
88 (ex 6), 92, 98, 99; Nick Hawken p. 68-69; Ben Kirchner/Heart p. 14 (all),
17, 19, 25 (ex 5), 29, 37, 51, 53, 54, 55 (ex 7); Kveta/Three in a Box pp. 81 (ex
2), 87; David Oakley/Arnos Design pp. 16 (maps), 24 (maps), 66, 67, 79, 80;
Kim Smith/Eastwing pp9, 22, 23, 27 (ex 9), 48, 55 (ex 8, ex 11)

Commissioned Photography by: Chris King: cover, pp. 6 (ex 2), 7, 8, 10, 11, 13,
18, 19, 21, 30, 31, 33, 38, 39, 41, 46, 47, 49

*The publishers would like to thank the following for their kind permission to reproduce
photographs and copyright material*:
Alamy pp. 4, 6 (ex 4), 26, 44 (cooking empanadas), 75 (boy on phone), 79, 86
(valley, island, flamingos), 98; Art Directors/TRIP pp. 14, 32; Betws-y-
coed.com p. 29 (house); Chris Bonnington p. 36 (climber); Bubbles p. 89 (girl
on phone); Collections p. 35; Corbis pp. 16 (Scott Expeditionary team), 29
(boy), 57, 62 (Temba Tsheri Sherpa), 84, 93; Eurochocolate p. 44; Eye
Ubiquitous p. 64 (1000 year old eggs); Florida Strawberry Festival p. 44;
FLPA p. 63 (shark with open mouth); Getty pp. 4 (girl in restaurant), 15, 57,
65 (aterial nanobot), 73, 89 (Patagonia), 90 (Tierra del Fuego); Noel Hamilton
p. 63 (Bethany smiling); Katz p. 36 (Everest); Hulton Archive p. 16
(Magellan); OUP pp. 31, 63 (shark), 94; Panos Pictures p. 64 (man eating spider); Photofest p. 20; Powerstock/Superstock p. 86 (beach); Punchstock
29 (girl), 75 (teen girl); Rex Features pp. 29 (Burgh Island), 36 (rubbish), 42,
43, 44 (cheese rolling), 63 (Bethany surfing); Royal Geographical Society pp.
12, 36 (Hilary and Tenzing); Science Photo Library p. 64 (witchetty grub), 65
(DNA nanobots); US Navy Historical Center p. 24.

*We are also grateful to those who have given permission to reproduce the following
extracts and adaptations of copyright material*:

p 98 *Cry Me a River* Words and Music by Justin Timberlake, Scott Storch and
Timothy Mosley, copyright © Tennman Tunes, TVT Music Inc and Virginia
Beach Music, USA, Warner/Chappell Music Limited and EMI Music Publishing
Limited, London, WC2H 0QY 2002, reprinted by permission International
Music Publications Limited and BMG Music Publishing International Limited.
All Rights Reserved.

p 99 *Dancing in the Moonlight* Words and Music by Kelly Sherman, copyright
© EMI Catalogue Partnership, EMI U Catalog Inc, EMI United Partnership
Limited and St. Nathanson Music Limited, USA, worldwide print rights
controlled by Warner Bros. Publications Inc/IMP Ltd 1970, reprinted by
permission of International Music Publications Limited. All Rights Reserved.

p 100 *Sunshine on a Rainy Day* Words and Music by Zoe Pollock/Martin Glover
(E G Music and Zoe Pollock Music, 1994), reprinted by permission of MCS Plc
and Music Sales Limited. All Rights Reserved.

p 101 *The Tide Is High Words* and Music by John Holt, Howard Barrett and
Tyrone Evans, copyright © The Sparta Florida Music Group Limited 1968 &
1972, reprinted by permission of Music Sales Limited. All Rights Reserved.
International Copyright Secured.

With additional thanks to: Davenant Foundation School, The Globe Theatre,
Windsor Leisure Centre.

IRREGULAR VERBS

base form	past simple	past participle	base form	past simple	past participle
be	was / were	been	know	knew	known
become	became	become	learn	learnt, learned	learnt, learned
begin	began	begun	leave	left	left
bite	bit	bitten	lend	lent	lent
break	broke	broken	let	let	let
bring	brought	brought	lose	lost	lost
build	built	built	make	made	made
burn	burned, burnt	burned, burnt	meet	met	met
buy	bought	bought	pay	paid	paid
catch	caught	caught	put	put	put
choose	chose	chosen	read	read	read
come	came	come	ride	rode	ridden
cost	cost	cost	ring	rang	rung
cut	cut	cut	run	ran	run
do	did	done	say	said	said
draw	drew	drawn	see	saw	seen
dream	dreamt	dreamt	sell	sold	sold
drink	drank	drunk	send	sent	sent
drive	drove	driven	shine	shone	shone
eat	ate	eaten	shut	shut	shut
fall	fell	fallen	sing	sang	sung
feed	fed	fed	sit	sat	sat
feel	felt	felt	sleep	slept	slept
fight	fought	fought	speak	spoke	spoken
find	found	found	spend	spent	spent
fly	flew	flown	stand	stood	stood
forget	forgot	forgotten	steal	stole	stolen
freeze	froze	frozen	swim	swam	swum
get	got	got	swing	swung	swung
give	gave	given	take	took	taken
go	went	been / gone	teach	taught	taught
grow	grew	grown	tell	told	told
have	had	had	think	thought	thought
hear	heard	heard	throw	threw	thrown
hit	hit	hit	wake	woke	woken
hold	held	held	wear	wore	worn
hurt	hurt	hurt	win	won	won
keep	kept	kept	write	wrote	written